Eat Grub

Frances Lincoln Limited
74–77 White Lion Street
London N1 9PF

Eat Grub
Copyright © Frances Lincoln Limited 2016
Text © Grub (Shami Radia, Neil Whippey and
Sebastian Holmes) 2016
Food photography © Mowie Kay 2016
Design: Glenn Howard
Commissioning editor: Zena Alkayat

Travel photography © Tang Chhin Sothy/AFP/
Getty Images p10 left; © Dave Stamboulis/
Getty Images p10 right; © Eric-Paul-Pierre
PASQUIER/Gamma-Rapho via Getty Images
p13 left; © Wolfgang Kaehler/LightRocket via
Getty Images p13 right; © AP Photo/Apichart
Weerawong p182 left; © Hoang Dinh Nam/AFP/
Getty Images P182 right.

First Frances Lincoln edition 2016

A catalogue record for this book is available from
the British Library.

ISBN 978-0-7112-3694-3

Printed and bound in China

1 2 3 4 5 6 7 8 9

Quarto is the authority on a wide range of topics.

Quarto educates, entertains and enriches the lives of
our readers – enthusiasts and lovers of hands-on living.

www.QuartoKnows.com

Eat Grub

**THE ULTIMATE
INSECT COOKBOOK**

SHAMI RADIA AND NEIL WHIPPEY
RECIPES BY SEBASTIAN HOLMES

FOOD PHOTOGRAPHY BY MOWIE KAY

FRANCES
LINCOLN

Contents

About Grub

To explain how this cookbook came about, we need to explain why two ordinary guys decided to set up a company to bring edible insects to Western diners. Grub was launched by me (Shami Radia) and my good friend Neil Whippey following a (slightly drunken) conversation on his 30th birthday. We couldn't understand why nearly half the world's population ate insects, while the other half found the very idea revolting.

Grub founders Neil Whippey (left) and Shami Radia

Before setting up Grub in 2014, I worked for an international development charity, which would take me to remote and wonderfully unique countries. They each had their local delicacies, and some of those included insects. On my visits, I took pride in being happy to eat everything that was offered to me. It would have felt impolite to say no to food that someone had especially prepared – besides, if it's a meal they enjoy eating, why wouldn't I? As it turns out, many of the insect dishes were absolutely delicious and really satisfying.

Despite this culinary experimentation, the idea of launching Grub only took shape after I read an article in *National Geographic* about how sustainable and eco-friendly insects are to farm, and how little impact they have on land (unlike traditional farming). Neil was interested in a different element of the article, which explained how nutritious insects can be.

When he was 18 years old, Neil was diagnosed with the debilitating autoimmune illness Crohn's disease. He'd struggled in his early adult life to manage the weight loss and cramps that came with it, and spent years looking for nutritional ideas to help keep him healthy. He finally found something that could help supplement his diet: insects. The amino acid profile and protein were fantastic additions to a balanced diet, and though it wasn't a cure (and might not have the same impact for everyone with Crohn's disease), eating insects gave him the nutritional boost he needed.

Tasty, eco-friendly, nutritious... what's not to love? It made total sense that insects should be embraced as food in the West. But both Neil and I understood it was going to be something of a challenge to change people's perceptions of eating insects. And Grub was created to tackle this challenge – and overcome it!

In order to fully take on the task, I quit my job and started travelling
to countries where entomophagy (insect-eating) is an everyday norm.
I wanted to research why people ate insects and how they prepared and
cooked them. Neil did the groundwork back at home, taking care
of the market research and setting up the company. It was a big step
for both of us. The only thing missing from our team was someone with
the confidence and imagination to show people how easy and tasty it
could be to cook with insects. But we were really lucky, finding talented
young chef Sebby (Sebastian Holmes) who was incredibly excited by the
prospect of cooking with a completely new ingredient. He brought the
mad creativity that only top chefs have and has proved insects aren't
just a worthy food source, they taste great too.

Grub grew far more quickly than any of us had anticipated. Our
insects (except for our own-farmed crickets) are reared in Holland for
human consumption, then freeze-dried to lock in flavour and make them
easy to cook with – and they were selling in big numbers. The first year
was an exciting blur: we were hosting sell-out tasting events, being
featured in mainstream press and seeing our insects be the first to be
sold in a UK supermarket. Sebby started to develop menus for Grub's
pop-up restaurants as well as products such as cricket nut fudge and a
range of roasted crickets, which were getting lots of repeat orders. Since
that first year, we've discovered the interest in eating insects isn't a fad,
it's growing rapidly. Grub's vision is for insects to be embraced as a tasty,
healthy food that's kind to our planet. We strongly believe that Western
countries will come to accept insects. We've always pointed to sushi as
an example of a culturally specific food that wasn't eagerly received at
first, but is now a normal part of our diet. We hope this book will help
inspire the insect-eating revolution, one delicious dish at a time...

What is entomophagy?

Entomophagy is derived from the Greek words 'entomon' (insect) and 'phagein' (to devour) – and the fact that it has its own term gives some indication of the importance and history of entomophagy. Cave paintings found in Spain dating from 30,000 to 9,000 BC show edible insects and their larvae, while early Biblical examples include John the Baptist surviving on a diet of honey and locusts.

Far left: Cambodian street vendors sort crickets (caught by farmers from Kampong Thom province) ready for sale at a market in Phum Thun Mong, Cambodia. Left: Fried insects at a market in Chiang Mai, Thailand

Basically, eating insects isn't a new phenomenon or novelty fad. In fact, insects are today commonly eaten in 80% of the world's nations. Roughly 2 billion people worldwide eat insects regularly – that means someone, somewhere is tucking into a tasty insect snack right now.

There are more than 1,900 species of insect that have been identified as edible to humans, but there are bound to be thousands more that we just haven't got around to trying yet. The most commonly eaten insects are crickets, grasshoppers, ants, beetles (and their larvae such as mealworms and buffalo worms), and several species of caterpillars (including mopani and bamboo worms).

Before setting up our edible insect company Grub, I went travelling around the world in search of traditional insect cuisine, and did plenty of research on insect-eating nations. I wanted to know who eats insects, which insects they eat, how they cook them and how they perceive them as part of their national cuisine. My journey took me to many remote and interesting places with cultures that have been embracing insect-eating for centuries, millennia even.

I discovered that in Mexico, 'chapulines' (grasshoppers) are an extremely popular ingredient, especially in Oaxaca City where they're fried (often with chilli) and eaten as an everyday snack by adults and children alike. In Japan, a favourite is the zazamushi (which literally translates to 'insect that lives at the bottom of a river'); it's cooked in sweet soy sauce and served with sake. And in southern African countries, mopani worms can demand a higher price (gram for gram) than beef. In Bali I ate boiled dragonflies in coconut milk with rice (cooked this way, they have a similar texture and taste to soft-shell crab). And in Thailand I visited a school where, during their lunch break, children caught crickets in UV traps set up around the grounds.

They'd then keep them to be cooked with pandanus leaves and pepper
as a mid-afternoon snack.

My strangest eating experience had to be in Cambodia in a town
called Skuon. This place is famous for its tarantula population and a
human population that like to catch and eat them (I'm aware that spiders
aren't insects, but they tend to be categorised within entomophagy).
The hunting technique is ancient and is still preserved today: a homemade
fishing rod (string on a stick) with honeycomb at the end is dangled
down tarantula holes. When the spider bites the honey it becomes stuck
and can be lifted out. The hunting is usually done by young children who
then sell the spiders at the market for pocket money. I admit to a mild
case of arachnophobia, so I was dreading the experience of tucking
into them as a meal. But I boldly bought a few beers and tray of
roasted tarantulas from the local market to share with my hosts – when
I saw them devour them with a dipping chilli sauce, I was encouraged.
I thought the legs tasted nice (a little like the crispy bit of a chicken
wing), but I struggled with the bloated abdomen which had the texture,
not the taste, of a profiterole. It sagged and then a bitter cream oozed
out – it was the part the locals enjoyed the most.

The fact that this tarantula abdomen was the locals' favourite bit
is quite revealing. One of the questions sceptics like to ask is: why eat
insects in the West when we have affordable meat? This is making the
assumption that people only eat insects because they can't afford pork,
beef or chicken. In reality, insects (or tarantula abdomens) are often
seen as a treat and a delicacy in these countries, not a food eaten out of
necessity. It is simply a learned behaviour to eat (or not to eat) insects.

The eating experiences I had abroad are just a few of the many ways
in which insects are enjoyed by different cultures around the world
today, some of which Grub believes can be easily adopted by our own
culture here in the West. Probably not the tarantulas, though – at least
not just yet.

We certainly hope that by making insects easy to buy (and taking the
fear out of knowing whether they're suitable for human consumption),
Grub is able to encourage people to try edible insects and experiment
with them in everyday cooking. If you want to give it a go, see **www.
eatgrub.co.uk** to buy insects, or see page 183 for more on farming and
sourcing insects.

The rise of insect eating

Insects are a normal part of the culinary landscape throughout much of the world. It's only in Europe and North America where insects are not commonly eaten – but this seems to be changing, fast. The debate on whether we should all be eating insects seems to be reaching fever pitch, with more and more Western chefs, scientists, food experts and ecologists getting on board with the idea of entomophagy.

You might have noticed the number of news reports on entomophagy increase over the past few years. Or perhaps you've heard about one of the world's most celebrated chefs, René Redzepi, experimenting with ants on his menu at Noma in Copenhagen. Redzepi even tasked the researchers at the Nordic Food Lab (an organisation he co-founded to investigate 'food diversity and deliciousness') to explore insect gastronomy. Edible insect companies have sprung up around the world, and now there is a business and brand for everything entomophagy-related, from cricket farms to cricket-flour protein bars.

This interest, buzz and entrepreneurship didn't happen overnight. Back in 2009, the UN Food and Agriculture Organization (UNFAO) started advocating a move towards eating insects. A global meeting in Chiang Mai in Thailand championed insects as the most viable alternative source of protein to meat because of their ecological friendliness. Often, it can take several years before what makes sense to scientists makes sense to (and is embraced by) the public at large. But people are starting to understand the considerable benefits. If you still need convincing, we've broken down the growing argument for eating insects here...

For starters, farming insects has many environmental advantages over rearing other animals for food. Farming insects creates significantly less greenhouse gas and ammonia than other livestock. Insects are also more very efficient at converting feed to protein because they are cold-blooded, so they don't need to burn calories to keep themselves warm. And they don't need anywhere near as much feed: to produce the same amount of protein, crickets consume 12 times less feed than cattle, four times less than sheep, and half as much as chickens.

But perhaps the biggest eco benefit is the preservation of water. Fresh water is the world's most precious resource and its increasing scarcity means that a barrel of it has at times demanded a higher price than oil. Agriculture, including the rearing of livestock, has been known to take priority over drinking water in some of the world's poorest countries. This shocking fact is even more shocking when you drill down into the statistics. Producing one kilo of grain-fed beef requires roughly 13,000 to 15,000 litres of fresh water – that's 2,100 litres for a 150-gram burger. In contrast, one kilo of cricket protein only requires eight litres of water. That's a huge difference!

But entomophagy isn't just about the environment. We often hear the term 'superfood' being bandied about, but insects really are just that, and people are cottoning on to their nutritious value. Insects are extremely high in protein: the freeze-dried crickets Grub sells contain 69% protein, and our buffalo worms are 56% protein. Compare this to chicken, which on average contains 30% protein (but is often the protein source of choice among gym-goers). Insects contain many or all of the nine essential amino acids (depending on which insect you're eating). For example, mealworms contain as much (gram for gram) omega 3 and 6 as fish such as tuna. Insects also contain vital minerals: cricket flour contains more calcium than milk and more iron than spinach.

There is a wealth of information out there on the eco and nutritional benefits of farming and eating insects, but we won't go on about that any more here. This book is all about getting you cooking insects and loving the taste. And that's why Grub focuses on providing simple and tasty recipes for insect beginners (or pros!), and we hope you find this cookbook an entomophagy inspiration.

About Sebastian Holmes

So far in my career as a chef, insects are my most exciting culinary adventure. Along with Thai cooking, working with and eating insects is one of the most fascinating ways of experiencing food I've ever come across. It's so exciting to be able to welcome new people to entomophagy and introduce this collection of some of my favourite insect recipes.

Grub chef Sebastian Holmes

One thing I've never understood is why people think of 'insects' as one entity. There are in fact 1,900 known edible insects on the planet, and each and every one has its own distinctive qualities and flavours. It's a whole new food world to explore and experiment with.

As a chef, it was easy to fall in love with the versatile nature of insects as cooking ingredients. I actually believe that they're one of the most overlooked and therefore wasted ingredients in the world today (in particular the Western world). So I was delighted when Neil and Shami invited me to the pub to talk about cooking with crickets, grasshoppers, mealworms and buffalo worms. A few bowls of insects sat on the table between us (confusing everyone else in the pub), but I was undaunted. I've always been passionate about cooking, and I love being creative in the kitchen, so having a new ingredient to play with was thrilling – as was the challenge of getting insect cuisine on the Western culinary map. Generally in cooking, I find myself intrigued by the unknown. I've often stumbled across things that I love, and then spent my time trying to perfect my knowledge of them – and it's especially exciting if it's an ingredient or style of food that not everyone in the world is familiar with.

I consider my career a long one, and in my heart I've been a chef since I was 13 years old, when I took work experience in kitchens near where I lived in Oxfordshire. Since then I've rarely been out of a kitchen. A little later I learned the intricacies of my trade by training in British and European restaurants. All of this early involvement gave me a real taste for the hustle and bustle of a professional kitchen and from a very early age I knew I wanted to be a chef. In 2008 I went on a culinary odyssey, travelling to Thailand, Australia, New Zealand and Fiji to experience the culture and food.

On my return I managed to squeeze in another passion, and studied for a degree in journalism at Kingston University while simultaneously working in kitchens around London. When I graduated in 2012, I landed an amazing job in a cult Thai restaurant called The Begging Bowl in Peckham, London, learning from head chef Jane Alty (who worked with David Thompson at Nahm in Bangkok). It was here I learned to cook to an exceptionally high standard – I left three years later as sous chef having fallen totally in love with Thai cooking. I realised that Thai food is something I want to continue learning about for the rest of my life.

As well as moving on to work with Shami and Neil at edible insect company Grub, I left The Begging Bowl to become a head chef and launch Thai street food and barbecue restaurant The Smoking Goat in Soho, London. It was an instant hit, with round-the-block queues. Encouraged by the enthusiasm, I've now set up my own pop-up restaurant concept. The focus is on homemade Thai curries and noodles, all crafted from scratch.

All of this Thai experience (coupled with the fact that insects are a popular food in Thailand) will explain the many Asian influences in this book. But you'll also see South American flavours, British and American dishes, and European classics. Throughout, I've tried to make the dishes and ingredients as interesting and accessible as possible. In some cases, the insect is the star, in others it's there to add texture, flavour and protein. At the end, you'll find cocktail recipes by Grub friend Thom Lawson. Thom consults for numerous London restaurants and has a talent for designing bar menus and cocktails, even with insects.

Insects are a wonderful ingredient to work with and I hope the breadth of recipes in this book will inspire you to embrace insects in the kitchen, just as I've done.

Baked

Cooking Methods

Fried

Salts

Purées

Flours

Cooking with insects

Taking a bowl of insects and turning them into a meal may seem like a daunting task, but it's worth remembering that there's no real food culture or history of cooking with insects in the West. So of course we're all new and nervous when it comes to cooking with them.

The first time I was faced with insects as an ingredient, I had no idea what to do with them. I didn't even know how I was supposed to store them, let alone how to begin making them into a dish. However, through passion, trial and error (and a bit of obsessive practice), I began to work things out. Which insects go with which flavours, how the textures impact the final dish, how to prepare them and how to cook them so they don't end up tasting like dust.

Don't get me wrong, it wasn't always an easy journey: chowing down on burnt crickets – or worse, just ending up with a well-cooked dish that didn't taste good – was hard to swallow as a trained chef. But we all have to start somewhere when cooking with a new ingredient, and I hope that this book helps you to skip a few of the mistakes that I made. In fact, these recipes will help you put tasty dishes straight on to the table.

Throughout the book, the recipes I've written are based on five essential insect preparation and cooking methods. Each of these methods can be applied to any of the insects used in the book (except for ants – they don't require any preparation). The way you choose to prepare certain insects for certain recipes depends entirely on the way in which you want the final dish to turn out. Just think about insects like potatoes: you can mash, roast, boil or fry them, but you choose the method of cooking depending on the dish.

On the following pages you'll find information on how to bake, fry and purée insects, as well as how to turn them into salts and flours ready to be incorporated into marinades and baking.

Insect flour

All the insects in the book can be made into flour. Cricket flour is a personal favourite of mine because it's so versatile to cook with and has a really exciting flavour. Use it in baking and it takes on a slight cocoa powder quality, while in some savoury recipes it has a subtle shrimp flavour, which can really bring a dish to life.

It's incredibly easy to turn insects into flour and the method is the same for each of the insects in this book. Start by dry-roasting them in a pan over a medium heat for about 4–6 minutes, moving them with a spoon regularly. When they turn a golden brown colour, turn off the heat.

You then need to make the roasted insects into a powder. You can use a mortar and pestle to grind them, or use a spice grinder to achieve a fine powder. 1 gram of insects makes 1 gram of flour, though if you're measuring them out for a recipe add a few more insects, as you might lose some flour in the grinder. Or make up a big batch – the flour can be stored in a cool, dry place for up to 9 months.

If you want to experiment with flavours, you can add spices to the pan at the dry-roasting stage. For example, star anise or cinnamon with crickets is a great combination when baking desserts.

Insect flour can be used in many dishes that traditionally call for plain flour. However, it contains no gluten and no raising agents. If you mix insect flours with more traditional flours you will still get a rise in the bake while keeping the flavour of the insect. In my experience, 1 part insect flour to 2 parts traditional flour works best for breads and cakes.

Insect purées

Insect purées are very easy to make and also very versatile to use in dishes – they often form the base for sauces, jams and marinades (as you'll see throughout the book).

For a basic purée, add the insects to a saucepan and cover with vegetable stock. Don't add too much stock, just enough to cover them. Simmer over a medium heat for 8–25 minutes until they have softened (this depends on how hard the insect is, so keep checking). At this point, they should have taken on the flavour of the stock. If the stock evaporates, top up with a little more so the pan doesn't boil dry.

Transfer to a food processor (or use a hand-held blender) to make a paste. You may want to add more stock or water to reach the consistency you're after. The thicker the purée, the more intensely insect-flavoured it will be.

Of course, instead of using vegetable stock to simmer the insects in, you can use any liquid to make a purée. Or you can soften the insects by simmering, then draining and adding oils and spices before blending to create a paste. Just be brave and experiment!

Insect purées are a beginner-friendly way of introducing insects into your diet. Firstly, purées make insects easier to include into dishes that you eat every day, and secondly, they take away the fear some people have of eating insects in their whole form. In a purée, you can taste the insect without having to face it.

Insect salts

Making an insect salt is a similar process to making insect flour (see page 24). It's very simple to do with all of the insects in this book.

First, dry-roast the insects in a pan over a medium heat for 5-6 minutes. They'll turn a golden brown colour, at which point turn off the heat. If you're feeling creative, you can dry-roast the insects with herbs and spices, such as chillies, black pepper, paprika or thyme to give them an extra kick of flavour.

Once dry-roasted, grind them (along with any herbs or spices) to a fine powder in a spice grinder (or use a mortar and pestle), then add the salt. A good ratio is 1 part fine salt to 5 parts ground insects. 1 gram of insects makes 1 gram of ground insects, though if you're measuring them out for a recipe add a few more insects as you might lose a little in the grinder.

Once you've made up a insect salt mixture, you can store it in a cool, dry place for up to 9 months and just use when needed.

The salt enhances the flavour of the insect, rather than disguising it. Combining the insects with the salt allows you to incorporate the flavour of the insect into any dish you would normally add salt to (ie, everything!).

If using insects for the first time, or serving them to friends and family for the first time, this is a good place to start. See page 62 for an interesting salts tasting platter.

Fried insects

Deep-frying is the most common insect-cooking method around the world. In Asia, people often snack on fried insects coated in fish sauce, chilli powder or white pepper.

I do agree (with the world) that deep-fried insects are delicious, and if it's your first time cooking with insects then frying them should be one of the methods you try. However, I do find that it limits how creative you can be with them, and it's not the healthiest of cooking methods – which is a shame given how healthy insects are.

Insects are deep-fried in much the same way as onions are. Heat enough rapeseed oil for deep-frying (about 1 litre/1¾ pints/4 cups oil) into a deep heavy-based pan over a high heat until it reaches 180°C/350°F, or until a cube of bread browns in 30 seconds. Once the oil is hot, carefully add the insects and stir so they're coated in the oil then deep-fry until golden brown. Crickets and grasshoppers will fry in 30–40 seconds, mealworms will be done in 20–30 seconds and buffalo worms will be golden brown in 10–20 seconds. Once they are cooked, remove with a slotted spoon and drain on kitchen paper.

The process of frying insects in oil will make them crispy – so this is a great technique if you want to give a recipe a bit of crunch. You can also fry insects in flavoured oil, such as chilli oil or garlic oil – they then take on all of that flavour, making a more exciting taste experience.

Baked insects

Baking with insects is relatively easy. They can either be baked whole as part of a larger dish or ground into flour. I've found the latter to be the best method for baking insects, as flours tend to get more out of the insects in terms of flavour and protein (see page 24 for instructions on how to make insect flour).

For me, mealworms and buffalo worms are the best insects to bake whole as they have a particular ability to take on the flavour of other ingredients while baking. Add them to flapjacks for an added nutty bite, or to pasta bakes in place of meat – or even as a crunchy topping instead of breadcrumbs.

If you're roasting them on a baking tray, preheat the oven to 180°C/350°F/gas mark 4. Grasshoppers take 8 minutes to roast; crickets take 5 minutes; and buffalo and mealworms take 3 minutes to roast. You can bake them with herbs, spices or even a little chilli oil and add them to soups and salads as a topping. And you can roast them for longer if you want a crispy finish.

If you're baking with an insect flour, the general rule of thumb when experimenting with a new recipe is to use 1 part insect flour to 2 parts traditional flour (see page 24). Just remember that insects do not work as setting or raising agents. So you can't replace self-raising flour with cricket flour completely, but you can add it for taste and protein.

Baking with insect flour is an exciting way to explore the scope of insect dining. So many of the dishes we eat on a daily basis contain flour, and you can make them all with insect flour.

Tasting notes

Mealworms are oaty on first bite, with a subtle hint of seeds. They work in flapjacks and blitzed up in a protein shake.

Length 20-24mm/¼-1 inch

Nutritional value per 100g of freeze-dried product

Energy (kcal): 550

Fat (g): 37.2, of which saturates (g): 9.0

Carbohydrates (g): 5.4, of which sugars (g): trace

Fibre (g): 6.5

Protein (g): 45.1

Salt (g): 0.37

Mealworms are 45% protein and low in fat – the perfect light snack. They taste a little like almonds. Try roasting them on a tray with some garlic at 180°C/350°F/gas mark 4 for 3 minutes, then sprinkle on your soup or salad.

Mealworms

Buffalo worms

Buffalo worms are 56% protein, and have a distinctive nutty flavour. Try them lightly pan-fried in a little oil with some chilli for a few minutes (until they turn golden brown). Eat as a snack alongside an ice-cold beer.

Tasting notes
Buffalo worms start with a light, almost mushroom-like taste, which develops, becoming sweeter, then finishes with a strong walnut flavour.

Length 12-14mm/½ inch

Nutritional value per 100g of freeze-dried product

Energy (kcal): 484

Fat (g): 24.7, of which saturates (g): 8

Carbohydrates (g): 6.7, of which sugars (g): trace

Fibre (g): 5.2

Protein (g): 56.2

Salt (g): 0.38

Tasting notes
These are light and crisp, with a very
gentle nutty flavour. They work very
well in stir-frys.

Length 40-45mm/1½-1¾ inches

Nutritional value per 100g of freeze-dried product
....
Energy (kcal): 559
....
Fat (g): 38.1, of which saturates (g): 13.1
....
Carbohydrates (g): 1.1, of which sugars (g): trace
....
Fibre (g): 8.4
....
Protein (g): 48.2
....
Salt (g): 0.43
....

*Gram for gram, grasshoppers contain as much protein as beef.
They are 48% protein. Try dipping in tempura batter and deep-
frying, then serve with sweet chilli sauce.*

Grasshoppers

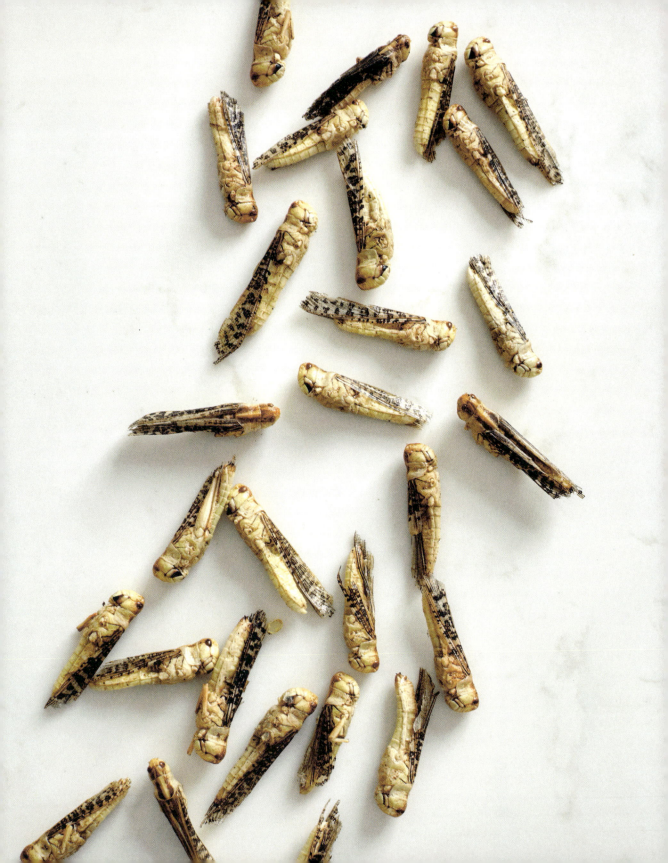

Crickets are high in minerals including iron and calcium. They are 69% protein. Coat in soy sauce and roast at 180°C/350°F/gas mark 4 for 5 minutes. Once they turn crispy, sprinkle with a pinch of white pepper and chilli powder for a great snack.

Crickets

Tasting notes
Crickets have the meatiest flavour of the four insects used in this book. They have a subtle shrimp flavour, and can be rich and bacon-like when cooked in soy sauce.

Length 18-20mm/¾ inch

Nutritional value per 100g of freeze-dried product

Energy (kcal): 458

Fat (g): 18.5, of which saturates (g): 7.0

Carbohydrates (g): 0, of which sugars (g): trace

Fibre (g): 7.7

Protein (g): 69.1

Salt (g): 1.03

Snacks

Crispy crickets and pandanus leaves

This is a really common snack in Thailand – in some areas it's even served to children as part of a school dinner. It's one of Grub's favourite recipes because it's quick and easy to prepare, and packs in a lot of cricket flavour.

Serves 2–3

- 1 litre/1¾ pints/4 cups vegetable oil, for deep-frying
- 200g/7oz crickets
- 3 pandanus leaves, chopped into big chunks
- 3 tbsp light soy sauce
- ground white peppercorns, enough to coat the crickets and leaves

01 First, heat the oil in a wok or deep saucepan to 160°C/325°F, or until a cube of bread browns in 30 seconds. When hot, carefully drop in the crickets and pandanus leaves and deep-fry for about 30–40 seconds, or until the insects and leaves are crunchy.

02 Remove the crickets and leaves with a slotted spoon and leave to drain on kitchen paper.

03 Put the soy sauce in a bowl and spread the ground white peppercorns out on a plate. Place the insects and pandanus leaves first in the soy sauce and then toss them in the pepper until they are lightly coated. Serve.

Buffalo worm and venison jerky with sour chilli dipping sauce

This jerky has a deep, rich flavour and lots of added protein. It's a simple twist on a classic beef jerky and it makes an excellent sharing snack – just top with crispy fried shallots for some extra crunch and serve with an ice-cold beer.

Serves 1-2

- ¾ tsp salt
- 10g/⅓oz buffalo worms
- 4 garlic cloves, peeled
- 50ml/1¾ fl oz/scant ¼ cup oyster sauce
- 2 tsp coriander seeds, toasted
- 300-400g/10½-14oz venison steak, sliced into thin strips, about 5mm/ ¼ inch thick

For the sour chilli sauce

- 200g/7oz long red chillies
- 50g/1¾oz/¼ cup palm sugar, or soft brown sugar works well too
- 2 tbsp fish sauce
- 150ml/5fl oz/⅔ cup distilled white vinegar
- 2 tbsp olive oil
- 200ml/7fl oz/scant 1 cup oyster sauce

01 Using a mortar and pestle or food processor, pound or blitz the salt, buffalo worms and garlic to a fine paste. Transfer to a shallow dish and add the oyster sauce and toasted coriander seeds. Add the meat and toss until it is coated all over. The seeds will stick to the meat.

02 Cover with clingfilm and allow to marinate for 2 –12 hours, depending on how much time you have.

03 In Asia the meat is dried quickly by leaving it in the sun, but if you don't have the luxury of hot sun there are other ways. For best results, place the meat on a baking tray, cover with parchment paper and leave in a warm, dry place (such as an airing cupboard) overnight, or until dried. Or for fast results, place in an oven preheated to 80°C/175°F/ lowest possible gas mark for 3-4 hours. Check on progress regularly. The only downside to this method is the quick drying process discolours the meat a little - it still tastes the same though.

04 Meanwhile, make the sour chilli dipping sauce. On a chargrill or a hot pan, char the chillies until slightly blackened and soft. Next, remove the stems and place in a food processor with the sugar, fish sauce, vinegar, olive oil and oyster sauce and blitz until smooth. It should be orange-red in colour and taste sweet, salty, sour and hot.

When ready to serve, tear the meat up into bite-sized pieces and serve with the dipping sauce on the side. You can fry some thinly sliced shallots as well as some more buffalo worms in chilli oil, and sprinkle on top to garnish.

Red curry cricket rice cakes
with chilli and garlic dipping sauce

If you like to have snacks to hand, this is great as the rice cakes keep in the fridge for two to three days, and the sauce can be kept for a couple of months without losing its flavour. The cakes make use of the red curry paste recipe on page 129, or you can buy it pre-made from most supermarkets.

Serves 2

For the rice cakes

- 100g/3½oz/½ cup glutinous rice (sticky rice)
- 10g/⅓oz crickets, roughly chopped
- 30g/1oz/⅓ cup desiccated (dry unsweetened) coconut, toasted
- 40g/1½oz red curry paste (see p129)
- 150ml/5fl oz/⅔ cup fish sauce

For the chilli and garlic dip

- 500ml/17fl oz/2 cups vegetable oil, for deep-frying
- 25 garlic cloves, peeled
- salt
- 10–12 dried long red chillies, deseeded if you like a milder heat
- 3 slices ginger

To garnish

- a small handful of coriander (cilantro), roughly chopped
- a small handful of peanuts
- 1 long red chilli, sliced

01 You will need a rice steamer for this recipe. If you don't have one, use a vegetable steamer: just cover the large holes at the base of the steamer with clingfilm and make smaller holes in it with a fork. This creates a steamer that rice won't fall through. Soak the glutinous rice in a bowl of cold water for 12 hours in the fridge to soften.

02 The next day, drain the rice and mix with the crickets. Place in the rice steamer and steam for 30–35 minutes until it turns translucent and is soft to eat. Remove from the steamer, place in a bowl and allow to cool a little, but don't let it get cold.

03 While the rice is still warm, add the coconut, curry paste and fish sauce and mix well, then squeeze into evenly sized balls. Flatten each ball with the palm of your hand then set aside to cool.

04 Meanwhile, preheat the oven to 180°C/350°F/gas mark 4. When the balls are cooled, place on a non-stick baking tray and bake in the oven for 20–25 minutes until they are golden brown and hot throughout.

05 While they're cooking, you can make the chilli and garlic dip. Heat the oil in a deep pan to 160°C/325°F, or until a cube of bread browns in 30 seconds. Pound the garlic and a pinch of salt together in a mortar and pestle or food processor until it's chopped into even chunks, then deep-fry for 1–2 minutes until golden and fragrant. Remove with a slotted spoon and drain on kitchen paper. Repeat this process with the chillies and then the ginger. Remove and drain on kitchen paper.

06 When cool, pound the crispy garlic, chillies and ginger together in a mortar and pestle or food processor, adding a little of the deep-frying oil to bind it all together, and if needed, add a little more salt.

Serve the dipping sauce with the hot rice cakes, garnished with coriander, peanuts and chilli.

Mealworm flour tortilla chips with salsa

These chips are just as moreish as their cornflour counterparts and make for a tasty pre-dinner snack. Serve with fresh salsa and a sprinkling of salt.

Serves 2–3

- 100g/3½oz/scant 1 cup masa harina golden cornflour (cornstarch, or use cornmeal ground in a food processor)
- 50g/1¾oz/scant ¼ cup mealworm flour (see page 24)
- ½ tsp salt
- 100–115ml /3½–4fl oz/ scant ½–½ cup warm water
- olive oil, for sprinkling

For the salsa

- 2 beef tomatoes, stems removed, diced
- ½ red onion, diced
- 1 bird's eye (Thai) chilli, sliced
- juice of 1 lime
- 1 tsp chopped coriander (cilantro)
- a pinch of ground cumin
- salt and freshly ground black pepper, to taste

01 Preheat the oven to 180°C/350°F/gas mark 4. Mix both flours and ½ teaspoon salt together in a bowl while slowly adding the warm water until the mixture forms a ball of dough, then knead the dough ball until it's completely smooth.

02 Divide the dough into 8 small portions. Place a portion between 2 pieces of parchment paper and roll out as thinly as possible, ideally 2mm/1/16 inch thick. Try to form an even disc. Set aside and repeat with the remaining portions.

03 Toast each rolled-out portion of dough in a dry, non-stick pan until golden brown on both sides, then cut the toasted dough into triangular sections and sprinkle lightly with olive oil and salt and pepper.

04 Place the tortillas on a non-stick baking tray and bake in the hot oven for 6–8 minutes until golden brown and crispy. Allow to cool.

05 Meanwhile, make the salsa. Place all the ingredients in a bowl, season with salt and black pepper and mix together.

Serve, sprinkled with a little salt and the salsa on the side. These tortilla chips can be stored for 2–3 days in an airtight container in a cool place.

Sticky crickets

Sticky crickets have been a real favourite at our pop-up Grub events. It's a dish that seems to remind people of crispy Peking duck and pancakes: the sauce is rich and aromatic (much like hoi sin sauce) and the crickets have the same sweet and salty crunch of crispy duck. Just add slices of refreshing cucumber: it's a winning combination.

Serves 3–4 as a snack or starter

- 1 litre/1¾ pints/4 cups rapeseed (canola) oil, for frying
- 30g/1oz banana shallots, thinly sliced
- 200g/7oz/1 cup palm sugar or soft brown sugar
- 2 tbsp tamarind water (from Asian grocery stores)
- 2 tbsp fish sauce
- 2 tbsp soy sauce
- 15g/½oz crickets
- small piece of cassia bark or cinnamon stick
- 2 star anise
- 10g/⅓oz whole coriander seeds
- a small handful of coriander (cilantro) leaves
- 1 cucumber, chopped into dipping-size chunks

01 First, deep-fry the shallots. In a deep saucepan, heat the oil to 160°C/325°F, or until a piece of shallot bubbles a little when dropped in. Have a tray with kitchen paper at the ready for when the shallots are removed. Deep-fry all the shallots in the hot oil for about 4–5 minutes, or until golden brown. Remove with a slotted spoon and drain on the kitchen paper.

02 Gently melt the palm sugar, tamarind water, fish sauce and soy sauce in a pan, stirring regularly until combined.

03 Meanwhile, toast the crickets, cassia bark, star anise and coriander seeds in another pan over a medium heat for 3–4 minutes until they all are evenly toasted, then add these to the palm sugar pan. Gently bring this mixture to the boil and then allow to bubble until the mixture thickens to a dipping consistency and reaches about 112°C/234°F in temperature. Take the pan off the heat and allow to cool until it is hot enough to eat.

Serve the sticky crickets scattered with the crispy shallots, coriander leaves and cucumber chunks for dipping.

Grasshopper and maltose porridge

Warm up some sweet, cinnamon-spiced porridge oats and top with sticky maltose grasshoppers for a truly hearty breakfast or downright indulgent snack. Add some fresh fruit to sweeten the treat – my favourites are strawberries and blueberries, but any will do.

Serves 1

- 40g/1½oz/½ cup porridge (rolled) oats
- 300ml/10fl oz/1¼ cups milk
- 2 heaped tbsp maltose
- 4 grasshoppers
- a small handful of blueberries
- a pinch of ground cinnamon

01 Heat the porridge oats and milk in a saucepan over a medium heat, stirring regularly.

02 Meanwhile, heat the maltose in another pan over a medium heat. Once hot and loose, add the grasshoppers and continue to heat, allowing the maltose to bubble and caramelise around the grasshoppers. It will thicken as it cooks. Once the grasshoppers are sticky and caramelised, about 3 minutes of boiling, roughly 115°C/239°F in temperature, they are ready to serve.

03 Once the oats have been simmering in the milk they will start absorbing the liquid. Take off the heat before all the milk has been absorbed, as it will continue to cook as you take it to the table.

Top the oats with the caramelised grasshoppers, the blueberries and a sprinkle of ground cinnamon and serve.

Cricket flour protein shake

Gram for gram, crickets have more protein than steak, making them an ideal addition to a protein shake. They also taste fantastic blitzed up with bananas and strawberries, though you can use your favourite fruits. You can add or omit the ice cream depending on whether this is a naughty drink or good old gym fuel.

Serves 2

- 3 bananas, peeled
- 200g/7oz/scant 1½ cups strawberries
- 1.2 litres/2 pints/5 cups milk
- 30g/1oz/scant ¼ cup cricket flour (see page 24)
- a scoop of vanilla ice cream, if you are feeling decadent

01 Blend everything together in a blender and drink away. If you fancy a treat, add a scoop of vanilla ice cream to the blender then blend until everything is smooth.

George's mealworm bread

Dr George McGavin is an Honorary Research Associate at Oxford Museum of Natural History – and we have a mutual passion for cooking with insects. George has been studying entomology for much of his life and actually farms his own mealworms. I cooked a few of my recipes for him and, in return, he has been kind enough to share this mealworm bread recipe. Thanks George, it really is divine...

Makes 1 loaf

- 350g/12oz/3 cups granary flour or strong wholewheat flour, sifted, plus extra for dusting
- 150g/5½oz/1¼ cups mealworm flour (see page 24), sifted
- 7g/¼oz sachet fast-action dried (active dry) yeast
- 1 tsp salt
- 300ml/10fl oz/1¼ cups warm water
- 2 tbsp olive oil
- 1 tbsp clear honey

01 Place the flours, yeast and salt in a large bowl and mix together with your hands. Stir in the warm water with the oil and honey until combined to make a soft dough.

02 Turn the dough on to a lightly floured surface and knead for 5 minutes, or until the dough no longer feels sticky, sprinkling with a little more flour if you need to.

03 Oil a 500g/1lb 2oz loaf tin and put the dough in the tin, pressing it in evenly. Put the tin in a large plastic food bag, or wrap tightly with clingfilm and leave to rise in a warm place for 1 hour, or until the dough has risen to fill the tin and it no longer springs back when you press it with your finger.

04 Preheat the oven to 180°C/350°F/gas mark 4. Make several slashes across the top of the loaf with a sharp knife, then bake in the hot oven for 30–35 minutes, or until the loaf has risen and is golden brown.

05 Once cooked, remove the loaf from the tin and place on a wire rack. Tap the base of the bread to check that it's cooked: it should sound hollow. Allow to cool before serving.

Once baked, this can be treated like any other type of bread. It's best eaten within a few days of making and should be stored in a cool, dry place. It also freezes well.

Small plates

Insect chilli salts with sour fruits

This is a particularly good dish for demonstrating the range of flavours that insects have to offer – the chilli mix that the ground insects are combined with really helps to emphasise each individual taste.

Serves 2-3

- 2g grasshoppers
- 2g crickets
- 2g buffalo worms
- 1 red bird's-eye (Thai) chilli, optional
- ¼ tsp dried chilli powder
- 1 tsp caster (superfine) sugar, plus a little more if needed
- 2 tsp fine salt
- 1 green mango, peeled and sliced
- 1 guava, peeled and sliced
- Thai basil leaves (ordinary basil works too)

01 There's a full explanation of how to make insect salts on page 26, but if you're making several at once (as with this recipe) it's easier to do them all in the oven preheated to 180°C/350°F/gas mark 4. Keep them separate from each other on a non-stick baking tray and add them one at a time based on the cooking times as follows: grasshoppers take 8 minutes to roast; crickets take 5 minutes; and worms take 3 minutes to roast. Once roasted keep the insects separate and individually grind each one to a fine powder in a spice grinder.

02 To make the chilli mix for the salt, combine the fresh chilli, chilli powder, sugar and salt together in a bowl.

03 Distribute the chilli mix evenly between the 3 different ground insects. Combine well. These are now ready to eat, but if they are too hot for you then add some more sugar to cool down the spice.

Dip the fruit into the salts and enjoy. The Thai basil adds an aniseed flavour to this dish which really complements the insect salts. Store the salts in a cool dry place.

Double cheese mealworm rarebit with soft-boiled duck egg

The rich depth of flavour of blue cheese is surprisingly successful coupled with mealworms. This dish is perfect if you have guests coming for lunch as the rarebit element can be prepared well in advance.

Serves 3

- 100g/3½oz/scant 1 cup cheddar cheese, grated
- 100g/3½oz/scant 1 cup blue cheese, grated
- 100ml/3½fl oz/scant ½ cup milk
- 1 tbsp English mustard
- 2 tbsp Worcestershire sauce
- 30g/1oz mealworms
- 1 egg
- 1 egg yolk
- 1 tsp thyme leaves
- 1 tbsp cayenne pepper
- 3 duck eggs
- a loaf of your favourite bread
- a pinch of salt and ground black pepper

01 First, line a baking tray with parchment paper. Now move on to make the rarebit. In a small pan, melt the cheeses, milk, mustard and Worcestershire sauce over a low heat. Once melted, add the mealworms, egg and yolk. Throw in the thyme leaves, stir and then pour on to the parchment paper. Sprinkle with cayenne pepper and allow to set.

02 Have a large bowl of cold water with ice cubes at the ready. Bring a pan of salted water to a rolling boil (so it's bubbling). Place the duck eggs into the water and leave for 7 minutes. Carefully remove the eggs from the water and put into the bowl of ice-cold water to stop the cooking process. Once the eggs are cool enough to handle, delicately peel away the shells.

03 Once the rarebit has set, preheat the grill to medium. Cut the rarebit into rough squares and place as much as you like on top of slices of your favourite bread. Grill until the rarebit has melted and begun to brown.

04 To serve, slice off the tops of the eggs, sprinkle with salt and pepper and arrange mealworm rarebit alongside, ready for dipping.

Once the rarebit is made it can be kept in the fridge for 2–3 days. It's a perfect quick lunch.

Sage butter-fried potatoes and crickets

Even though this makes a good snack or side dish, be warned that crickets are incredibly filling! If you end up with more than you can eat, the dish keeps well in the fridge for one to two days.

Serves 2

- salt, a pinch
- 2 large potatoes, peeled and diced into even (ish) chunks
- 1 tsp finely chopped sage
- 50g/1¾oz/3½ tbsp butter, at room temperature
- a splash of rapeseed (canola) oil
- 20g/¾oz crickets
- 1 tsp torn basil leaves, to garnish
- a small handful of chives, roughly chopped, to garnish

01 Have a large bowl of cold water with ice cubes at the ready. Bring a medium saucepan of water to the boil then lower the heat to a simmer. Add a pinch of salt then add the diced potatoes and simmer for 6–8 minutes. Remove the potatoes and cool quickly in the bowl of ice-cold water. Once the potatoes are cooled, drain and set aside.

02 Put the chopped sage and warm butter in a bowl and mix well until combined. Set aside.

03 Next, heat a splash of oil in a frying pan over a medium-high heat. Once the oil is smoking hot, add the blanched potatoes and keep moving them around the pan every minute or so to allow the potatoes to brown. Once they are starting to brown, lower the heat to medium and add the crickets and most of the sage butter (set some aside for the garnish). Crickets take much less time to cook than potatoes and will immediately absorb the sage butter. Cook gently for 3–4 minutes until the potatoes and crickets are golden brown.

Finish by sprinkling over some ripped-up basil, salt and chives, if you like, and garnish with the sage butter you set aside earlier.

Chilli and lime buffalo worm oysters

Buffalo worms go beautifully with seafood and lime. Team this lovely summer dish with a couple of glasses of white wine, and enjoy in the garden.

Serves 2

- 1 tsp buffalo worms
- 1 tsp salt
- 2 garlic cloves
- a small piece of coriander (cilantro root; this is not essential but tastes good if you can get it)
- 3 green bird's eye (Thai) chillies
- 2 tsp caster (superfine) sugar
- juice of 5 limes
- juice of 2 mandarins
- 3–4 tsp fish sauce
- 6 oysters of local origin
- crushed ice, to serve, if you like
- 1 tsp dill leaves

01 First, dry-roast the buffalo worms in a pan over a medium heat for a few minutes. They'll turn a golden brown colour, at which point turn off the heat. Grind the buffalo worms and salt together in a spice grinder to make buffalo worm salt or use a mortar and pestle. Set aside.

02 Next, make the chilli and lime sauce. In a mortar and pestle or food processor, add the garlic and coriander root and pound or blitz to a paste. (You may need to use some of the salt as an abrasive to make the paste.) Add the chillies and continue to grind or pound until everything is combined and smooth. Add the sugar and continue to grind or pound to a paste.

03 Now add all the juice and fish sauce to the paste and adjust the seasoning to your taste. It should be sweet, salty, sour and hot. Set aside.

04 Next, shuck the oysters. Do this on a flat surface, flat side facing up. When looking down at the oyster one of the sides is known as the hinge side, as this is how the oyster holds the shell closed. It is this part of the oyster shell that needs to be opened using an oyster shuck, while holding the oyster in a tea towel in the other hand to make sure you don't slip and shuck yourself. Ease the oyster shuck into the gap in the shell until it releases slightly. At this point you can hinge the oyster free and take the shell off the top. Use a spoon to detach the oyster from the curved side of its shell; leave in the shell for easy eating.

Serve the oysters immediately on a bed of crushed ice, sprinkled with dill and the buffalo worm salt and drizzled with the chilli and lime dressing.

Creamy mealworm salt mussels

When buying mussels, remember to look out for pre-cleaned, de-bearded mussels – this saves a lot of time in the kitchen. Mop up the creamy broth with some of the mealworm bread on page 56.

Serves 2-3

- a little salted butter
- 2 garlic cloves, roughly chopped
- 1 white onion, diced
- 100ml/3½fl oz/scant ½ cup white wine
- 200ml/7fl oz/scant 1 cup vegetable stock
- 1kg/2¼lb fresh mussels, cleaned and de-bearded
- 150ml/5fl oz/⅔ cup double (heavy) cream
- 1 tsp chopped chives, plus extra to garnish
- 10g/⅓oz mealworms
- ½ tsp fine salt

01 This is a really quick dish to make. First, heat the butter in a pan over a medium heat and then begin frying the garlic and onion together. When they are beginning to brown, about 3-4 minutes, pour in the wine and bring to the boil. Lower the heat and simmer for a few minutes, stirring to loosen all the flavourful bits of onion and garlic that have stuck to the bottom of the pan.

02 Next, add the vegetable stock and bring to the boil. Add the mussels then cover with a plate or lid and leave for 2-3 minutes, carefully shaking once or twice. Once cooked all the mussels should be open – if they are not discard them.

03 Now, add the cream and chives and stir through gently.

04 Finally, dry-roast the mealworms in a pan over a medium heat for a few minutes. They'll turn a golden brown colour, at which point turn off the heat. Grind the mealworms and salt in a spice grinder or mortar and pestle to a powder, then sprinkle over the top of the mussels.

Garnish with more chopped chives and serve.

Curried beer tempura grasshoppers

People call grasshoppers the prawns of the sky! This is a play on that idea, and it's become one of the most popular dishes at Grub's pop-up restaurants. As well as being slightly shrimpy, grasshoppers have a gorgeous nutty flavour and this lightly curried tempura batter draws it out beautifully. Garnish with thinly sliced long red chillies and dip in sweet chilli sauce as a starter.

Serves 2–3, as a starter

- 20 grasshoppers, legs and wings removed
- a few splashes of light soy sauce

For the tempura batter

- 100g/3½oz/scant ⅔ cup white rice flour
- 2 tsp mild curry powder
- salt, a pinch
- 150ml/5fl oz/⅔ cup icy cold beer (freeze for 30 minutes before using)
- 1 egg, beaten
- 1 litre/1¾ pints/4 cups vegetable oil, for deep-frying

To garnish

- long thin red chillies, chopped
- a few deep-fried Thai basil leaves

01 First, dry-roast the grasshoppers. Preheat the oven to 180°C/350°F/ gas mark 4. Coat the grasshoppers in the soy sauce then put them in a baking dish, cover with foil and roast in the hot oven for 25–30 minutes. Uncover for the last 5 minutes to make the grasshoppers dry and crispy. Allow to cool.

02 Next, make the tempura batter. Sift the rice flour and curry powder together then add the salt. In another bowl, beat the cold beer and egg together until smooth and pale (the idea is to beat the bubbles out of the beer). Once smooth, add this wet mixture to the dry mixture and whisk together. Take care when whisking, as you don't want to overwork the gluten in the flour. When mixed to a smooth batter it's ready. (A few small lumps are fine.)

03 Meanwhile, heat the oil for deep-frying in a deep saucepan to about 170°C/338°F, or until a cube of bread browns in 30 seconds. Coat the roasted grasshoppers, one by one, in the rice flour mixture then, using chopsticks or tongs, dip them into the batter. Carefully drop them into the hot oil and deep-fry for about 20 seconds on each side until golden brown. Remove with a slotted spoon and drain on kitchen paper. The key to a good tempura is the cold beer batter plunging into the hot oil. The temperature change causes air bubbles in the batter to create more of a crunch when eaten.

Serve immediately, garnished with a few chopped chillies and deep-fried basil leaves, with sweet chilli sauce on the side if you like.

Tamarind, pomegranate and buffalo worm salad

Buffalo worms, peanuts and pomegranate give a satisfying crunch to this sweet and tart salad dish. Works well as a side dish, or light lunch.

Serves 2

For the dressing

- 300ml/10fl oz/1¼ cups vegetable oil, for deep-frying
- 2 garlic cloves, crushed
- 10g/⅓oz buffalo worms
- 80g/3oz/scant ½ cup palm sugar
- 200ml/7fl oz/scant 1 cup tamarind water (from Asian grocery stores)
- 40g/1½oz/¼ cup toasted peanuts, crushed or roughly chopped (if you cannot find toasted peanuts toast them yourself. Deep-fry in oil heated to 130°C/266°F until golden brown. Drain on kitchen paper)
- 80ml/3fl oz/scant ⅓ cup soy sauce

For the salad

- 1 pomegranate
- 100g/3½oz fennel bulb
- 30g/1oz cucumber
- 6 baby gem lettuce leaves
- 1 tsp roughly torn mint leaves
- 1 tsp coriander (cilantro) leaves
- 1 tsp toasted sesame seeds
- a small handful of Thai basil leaves, torn (ordinary basil works too)

01 Heat the vegetable oil in a small deep saucepan to 180°C/350°F or until a cube of bread browns in 30 seconds. Add the crushed garlic cloves to infuse the oil. Once the oil has reached temperature, carefully add the buffalo worms and deep-fry for 20–30 seconds until they are crunchy and infused with garlic. (They will stop making noise in the oil when they are ready as all the moisture will be extracted, making them crunchy.) When cooked, remove with a slotted spoon and drain on kitchen paper.

02 Heat the palm sugar and tamarind water together in another pan over a medium heat, stirring regularly to ensure the sugar does not stick to the pan. Once melted, add the peanuts and soy sauce then remove and allow to cool. Add the buffalo worms and check the seasoning as it may need some adjustment – it should taste sweet and sour with a savoury, salty edge.

03 Finally, prepare the vegetables and fruit for the salad. Slice the pomegranate in half across the core, then hit the skin side with a spoon to remove all the edible seeds. Remove the core and stems of the fennel and slice the flesh into bite-sized pieces. Slice the cucumber and baby gem lettuce to the same size and then combine in a large bowl with the mint and coriander. Add a generous helping of the salad dressing.

Serve topped with toasted sesame seeds and torn Thai basil.

Smoky cod and buffalo worm cakes

This recipe shows just how versatile insects can be. In this case, buffalo worms are used in both the main mix and the outer coating. The worms in the main fishcake remain moist and soak up the flavour of the other ingredients (although they still retain a flavour of their own), while the worms used in the crispy coating have a more distinctive taste.

Serves 2

- 500ml/17fl oz/2 cups milk
- 400g/14oz smoked cod
- 30g/1oz buffalo worms
- 2 potatoes, peeled and roughly chopped
- salt and black pepper, to taste
- 30g/1oz ginger, peeled and diced
- 20g/¾oz garlic, diced
- 4 tsp butter
- 2 egg yolks
- 4 tsp sweet chilli sauce
- 20g/¾oz/scant ½ cup dried breadcrumbs
- 20g/¾oz/scant ¼ cup plain (all purpose) flour

For the coating

- ½ tsp dried thyme
- ½ tsp dried rosemary
- 1 tsp smoked paprika
- ½ tsp ground cumin and ½ tsp cayenne pepper (or replace with 1 tsp Cajun seasoning)
- 10g/⅓oz dried buffalo worms
- 30g/1oz/scant ⅔ cup dried breadcrumbs
- 1 whole egg, beaten

01 Preheat the oven to 180°C/350°F/gas mark 4. Start by poaching the smoked cod and worms. To do this warm the milk in a pan over a medium-low heat then add the cod and worms and cook for 8–10 minutes until cooked through. Remove and set aside.

02 Meanwhile, boil the potatoes in another pan of salted water until soft. Drain thoroughly and mash to a smooth consistency with a potato masher.

03 Place the mashed potato, cod and worms in a large bowl with the ginger, garlic, butter, egg yolks, sweet chilli sauce, breadcrumbs and seasoning and mix thoroughly. Allow to cool and then either using a mould or your hands, shape the mixture into 4 cakes. Once shaped, coat the cakes lightly in the plain flour.

04 Next, mix all the ingredients for the coating together, except the egg, and spread out on a flat tray. If you like, you can used mixed herbs (instead of the thyme and rosemary) and Cajun seasoning in place of the paprika, cumin and cayenne pepper.

05 Using a brush or your fingers, coat the cakes, one by one, in the egg then add to the breadcrumb and spice mix and toss to coat. Repeat this process if the cakes are not completely covered.

06 To finish, cook the cakes in the hot oven for 15–20 minutes. The cakes are ready when they are piping hot inside and golden brown on the outside.

This is superb served on a bed of rocket leaves with a squeeze of lemon.

Crispy vermicelli noodle salad with yellow bean, lime and buffalo worm sauce

Now this is a slightly difficult dish to pull off – but if you're careful not to scramble the eggs when making the sauce, you should be fine. It's a really exciting Thai-inspired combination of ingredients, and they can all be found in a good Asian supermarket.

Serves 2–3

- 50g/1¾oz buffalo worms
- 100g/3½oz yellow bean sauce (soybean sauce)
- 1 litre/1¾ pints/4 cups rapeseed (canola) oil to fry the noodles, plus a further 150ml/ 5fl oz/ ⅔ cup, to cook the sauce
- 80g/3oz banana shallots, thinly sliced
- 100g/3½oz/½ cup caster (superfine) sugar
- 3 eggs, lightly beaten
- 80g/3oz canned pickled garlic, peeled and chopped
- 100ml/3½fl oz/scant ½ cup lime juice
- 50ml/1¾fl oz/scant ¼ cup freshly squeezed mandarin juice
- 300g/10½oz dried vermicelli noodles
- 10g/ ⅓oz Chinese or ordinary chives, chopped
- 10g/ ⅓oz beansprouts
- 1 tsp coriander (cilantro) leaves
- 5g/⅛oz long red chilli, deseeded and finely chopped

01 First, whizz the buffalo worms and yellow bean sauce in a food processor to make a paste. Set aside.

02 Next, heat about 150ml/5fl oz/⅔ cup oil in a wok or large frying pan over a high heat. Once hot, add the sliced shallots and fry for a few minutes until they begin to go golden brown. Next, add the buffalo worm and yellow bean paste and continue to fry until it begins to darken and smell nutty. Add the sugar then lower the heat to medium and continue to fry until the mixture becomes shiny and glossy. At this stage take the mixture off the heat and, bit by bit, add some of the hot mixture to the beaten eggs in a heatproof bowl. Whisk constantly to avoid scrambling the eggs. Keep doing this until you have added half of the hot sauce to the eggs.

03 Now pour the egg sauce back into the rest of the hot mixture in the wok and continue to cook over a low heat for another 2–3 minutes until thick. Take off the heat and add the juice from the can of pickled garlic, the lime juice and the mandarin juice, then keep warm.

04 Meanwhile, deep-fry the vermicelli noodles. Heat the measured oil in a deep pan to 180°C/350°F, or until a cube of bread browns in 30 seconds. Once hot, place the dried noodles in small handfuls into the hot oil and deep-fry for 20–30 seconds. They will become larger straight away. Remove with a slotted spoon and drain on kitchen paper.

05 To finish, put all the ingredients into a large bowl, including the chives, beansprouts, coriander and chilli, and mix together.

Serve immediately. If left too long the noodles will become sodden with the sauce.

Josh's scrambled eggs, mullet roe and ants

How do you like your eggs in the morning? Creamy and topped with a handful of ants?
This take on classic eggs-on-toast was masterminded for this book by Josh Pollen, co-founder
of culinary collective Blanch & Shock. He's pretty experimental, so if you're after a slightly
less adventurous brunch, substitute the mullet roe for a side of smoked salmon and the
monk's beard for diced samphire, but keep those ants for their wonderful citrus flavour.

Serves 2

- 4 very fresh biodynamic or organic eggs
- 2 tsp salted butter, cut into small pieces, plus extra for spreading
- 1 tbsp crème fraîche
- 2 slices of toast
- 50g/1¾oz monk's beard (this Italian vegetable is incredibly seasonal: replace with samphire for a similar flavour)
- 25g/1oz bottarga di muggine (dried pressed grey mullet roe, often available in Italian delis)
- 5g/⅛oz wood ants (*Formica rufa*): these are best sourced from an experienced forager and should be frozen as soon as they're collected. Defrost and use without further preparation

01 Mix the eggs well before adding to a saucepan set on a heat diffuser with the heat as low as possible. Stir the eggs constantly with a silicone spatula until they start to thicken, about 10 minutes.

02 Add the butter and continue to stir the eggs for another 10 minutes. They will start to scramble. If large chunks are forming, take the pan off the heat and vigorously stir or whisk to break up the mixture.

03 Just before the eggs are cooked to your liking, add the crème fraîche and stir in. Toast and butter 2 thin slices of good bread.

04 Steam the monk's beard for 10 seconds over a small pan of fresh boiling water.

Serve the eggs on the bread, put the monk's beard on the eggs, grate the bottarga finely over the monk's beard and sprinkle the ants on top. The ants are citrussy in flavour and complete the dish brilliantly.

Grasshopper, prawn and ginger spring rolls

Grasshoppers pair up very well with prawns, especially in these simple-to-make spring rolls. They're a fantastic way of introducing your insect-cooking skills to friends: a familiar dish with prawns as the main event, but with grasshoppers adding a unique new flavour.

Serves 2-3

- 300g/10½oz cooked rice noodles
- 400g/14oz mixed vegetables, thinly sliced and separated (red pepper, beansprouts, carrots, shredded Chinese leaf (napa) cabbage, spring onions/scallions)
- 100g/3½oz cooked small peeled prawns (shrimp)
- 40g/1½oz grasshoppers, legs and wings removed
- 100g/3½oz cooked chicken or duck breast, shredded
- 2 garlic cloves, finely chopped
- 1 small piece wild ginger (kra chi is available in good Asian grocery stores, otherwise use normal ginger), finely chopped
- a tiny splash of light soy sauce
- Chinese five-spice powder, for sprinkling
- 8-10 sheets of filo (phyllo) pastry
- 1 egg, beaten
- sesame seeds, for sprinkling

01 Preheat the oven to 180°C/350°F/gas mark 4 and line a baking tray with parchment paper. Mix the noodles, vegetables, prawns, grasshoppers and chicken together in a large bowl. Add the garlic, ginger, soy sauce and a sprinkling of five-spice to the bowl and mix everything together well.

02 Cut the pastry into rectangles and lay on the work surface. Spoon the filling down the side of each sheet nearest to you, then fold over the sides and neatly roll up into a cigar shape. Seal the ends with a little of the beaten egg. Lift the spring rolls on to the lined baking tray, seam-side down, brush with a little more egg and sprinkle with sesame seeds, if you like.

03 Bake the rolls in the hot oven for 20–25 minutes, or until golden and crisp. Take out of the oven and leave until cool enough to handle.

These spring rolls are a great snack and perfect when served with a sweet chilli dipping sauce. Once the spring rolls are shaped they can be frozen and baked in the oven at a later date.

Large plates

Mealworm piri-piri whole chicken

Buffalo worm salt can be used in a variety of different ways. Here it's fused with a range of herbs and spices to create a delectable chicken marinade. If you use a spatchcocked chicken, try cooking this dish on a barbecue – a charcoal-kissed piri-piri chicken can't be beaten, so keep it in mind for a sunny day.

Serves 2–3

- 1 whole chicken, about 1.5kg/3¼lb
- 4 red bird's eye (Thai) chillies, chopped and deseeded if you don't like it too spicy
- 3 garlic cloves, crushed
- 2 tbsp buffalo worm salt (see page 26)
- 2 tsp sweet paprika
- 1 tsp smoked paprika, ½ tsp ground cumin ½ tsp cayenne pepper (or replace with 2 tbsp seasoning)
- 2 tbsp pink peppercorns
- 3 tbsp Worcestershire sauce
- 3 tbsp soy sauce
- 2 tbsp red wine
- 2 tbsp red wine vinegar
- 2 big squirts tomato ketchup
- 2 tbsp chopped parsley
- 3 tbsp salted butter
- 6 tbsp olive oil
- coriander (cilantro) leaves, to garnish
- lemon wedges, to serve

01 To spatchcock the chicken, flip it over so the backbone is facing upwards. Using a sturdy pair of scissors, cut either side of the backbone, then discard. Turn the chicken over and push down firmly on the breastbone to flatten out the bird. Make a few slashes in each leg joint.
02 Put the chillies and garlic in a food processor with the buffalo worm salt and whizz to a paste (or use a mortar and pestle). Add the rest of the ingredients, except the coriander and lemon wedges, and mix well, then smear over the chicken. Allow to marinate in the fridge for at least 1 hour, or overnight if you have the time.
03 When the chicken is ready to cook, preheat the oven to 180°C/350°F/gas mark 4. Place the chicken skin-side down in a roasting tin then roast in the centre of the hot oven for 15–20 minutes. Flip the chicken over and continue cooking for another 5–15 minutes until cooked through. Check the juices run clear with a skewer inserted into the thickest part of the meat, such as the thigh, to make sure it's cooked through.
04 To char the skin, heat the grill and cook for 5–10 minutes.

Garnish the chicken with coriander and serve with lemon wedges. It's great served with some grilled corn on the cob and rice.

Grasshopper, sweet potato and corn fritters

Grasshoppers are an excellent addition to a crispy fritter, particularly in this instance where their nutty undertones complement the sweet potato. These things are great fun to eat, so get your friends around, get stuck in and make a mess!

Serves 2

- 2 litres/3½ pints/8 cups rapeseed (canola) oil, for deep-frying
- 1 tbsp mild curry powder
- 1 tbsp rice flour
- salt, to taste
- 200ml/7fl oz/scant 1 cup sparkling water
- 2 eggs
- 6-8 grasshoppers, legs and wings removed
- 1 sweet potato, cut into julienne or shredded
- heaped ½ tsp white sesame seeds
- baby corn cobs, chopped into small chunks
- 1 tsp Thai basil leaves
- a small handful of coriander (cilantro) leaves
- 1 lime

01 Heat the oil in a deep saucepan to 180°C/350°F, or until a cube of bread browns in 30 seconds.

02 While the oil is getting hot, whisk the curry powder, rice flour, a pinch of salt, the sparkling water and the eggs together in a large bowl until it's pale. This is your batter. Cover with clingfilm and allow to rest in the fridge for a few minutes.

03 In another bowl, combine the grasshoppers, shredded sweet potato, sesame seeds, chopped baby corn and basil. Pour the batter over this mixture then, using your hands, mix together until everything is covered in the batter.

04 Now the fritters are ready to be cooked. However, if you throw the mixture in as is, it will break up and not cook together, so use a spider utensil (a large spoon with holes, usually used to remove ingredients that have been deep-fried) to gently lower handfuls of the fritter mixture, one at a time, into the hot oil. Deep-fry for about 2–3 minutes, moving them regularly to ensure an even cook. When ready, remove and drain on kitchen paper.

Serve the fritters garnished with some coriander leaves and a cheek of lime to squeeze over the top, and enjoy.

Tomato soup topped with chilli-roasted buffalo worms

The chilli-roasted buffalo worms on top of this sweet, smooth soup add a welcome crunch – in fact, the worms can be used to top all manner of dishes, as they're a brilliant hot and crispy garnish. Any tomatoes will do for the soup, but I find that a combination of plum and vine tomatoes give an especially juicy result.

Serves 2-3

- 2 large plum tomatoes
- 400g/14oz vine cherry tomatoes
- 2 leeks, roughly chopped
- 1 large white onion, roughly chopped
- 4 garlic cloves, roughly chopped
- 100ml/3½fl oz/scant ½ cup olive oil
- 1 bird's eye (Thai) chilli, roughly chopped
- 1 large red chilli, roughly chopped
- salt and freshly ground black pepper, to taste
- 40g/1½oz buffalo worms
- 500ml/17fl oz/2 cups vegetable stock
- 200ml/7fl oz/scant 1 cup double (heavy) cream

01 Preheat the oven to 200°C/400°F/gas mark 6. Place both types of tomatoes, the leeks, white onion, garlic and 4 teaspoons of the olive oil in a roasting tin and roast in the hot oven for 15–20 minutes until coloured.

02 Meanwhile, make the chilli oil. Add the rest of the olive oil to a food processor with the chillies and a pinch of salt and pepper and whizz to combine.

03 Place the buffalo worms on an oven tray and use the chilli oil to coat the worms. Roast them on the lowest shelf of the oven for about 8–10 minutes until they are light golden brown and smell nutty, then remove and set aside.

04 Once the vegetables are starting to colour in the roasting tin, transfer them to a deep pan. Pour in the stock and cream and, using a hand-held blender, blend until smooth. Alternatively, blend in a food processor.

Serve the soup in a bowl topped with the crispy buffalo worms and a little more chilli oil. It looks wonderful if you set some of the roasted vine cherry tomatoes aside after roasting them and then put them on top of the soup as a garnish.

Creamy mealworm and coconut noodles

Mealworms and coconut cream are a great match: the nuttiness of the worms is a natural partner to the smooth coconut, and the chilli really sets the dish off. Rustle this up if you're in a hurry, and enjoy hot or cold.

Serves 2-3

- 400g/14oz vermicelli noodles
- 20g/¾oz mealworms, blanched
- 30g/1oz red turmeric, peeled
- 30g/1oz garlic , roughly chopped
- 40g/1½oz piece ginger, peeled
- 10g/⅓oz red bird's eye (Thai) chilli
- 2 tbsp rapeseed (canola) oil
- 200ml/7fl oz/scant 1 cup chicken stock
- 200ml/7fl oz/scant 1 cup coconut cream
- 4 tsp soy sauce
- 2 tsp fish sauce
- 1 tbsp caster (superfine) sugar
- 20g/¾oz coriander (cilantro) leaves
- 20g/¾oz spring onions (scallions), sliced
- 60g/2¼oz Thai shallots, sliced
- 60g/2¼oz chives, sliced
- 1 lime

01 First, prepare the vermicelli noodles. These are sold dried in blocks of noodles folded together and are simple to cook. Soak them in cold water for about 30 minutes. When they loosen up and detach from one another, drain and set aside in a colander.

02 Next, pound the mealworms, red turmeric, garlic, ginger and chilli in a mortar and pestle to a coarse paste. A food processor can be used instead.

03 Heat the oil in a wok or deep pan over a high heat. Add the paste and fry, stirring constantly to avoid burning, for a few minutes until the paste begins to darken. Add the chicken stock, coconut cream, soy sauce, fish sauce and sugar then lower the heat to medium and add the noodles. Cook the noodles for about 3-4 minutes, or until they absorb the sauce and soften. To check if they are cooked, try some - the noodles should have a little bite, but be moist and soft in your mouth. If they are a little dry add a touch more coconut cream then take off the heat.

04 Finish the dish by mixing through the coriander, spring onions and Thai shallots.

Serve, garnished with chopped chives and a cheek of lime. The fresh acidity of the lime really lifts this dish; recommend to your fellow diners that they add a squeeze just before eating.

Roasted tomato and pancetta pizza with cricket flour dough

Cricket flour is fast becoming one of my favourite insect-based ingredients to cook with. It's such a versatile product, and this rosemary pizza dough is a prime example of why. It's super-easy to make, and the mixture rises fast so you'll have a slice in hand well before any home-delivered alternative.

Serves 2–3

- 250g/9oz/scant 2¼ cups plain (all-purpose) flour, plus extra for dusting
- 125g/4oz/scant ⅔ cup cricket flour (see page 24)
- 1 tsp salt
- 1 tbsp caster (superfine) sugar
- 1 tsp chopped rosemary leaves
- 7g/¼oz fast action dried (active dry) yeast
- 2 tbsp olive oil
- 225ml/8fl oz/1 cup warm water, about 45°C/113°F

For the topping

- 400g/14oz canned chopped tomatoes
- 2 garlic cloves, chopped
- salt and freshly ground black pepper, to taste
- 3 tbsp tomato purée (paste)
- 6 rashers (slices) of pancetta, chopped
- 200g/7oz/1¾ cups mozzarella cheese, torn up
- 8 vine cherry tomatoes, on the vine
- a handful of rocket (arugula)

01 First, make the dough. Combine the flours, salt, sugar, rosemary and yeast in a large bowl. Mix in the oil and warm water, then knead together with your hands until everything is combined and the dough is not sticky but soft to the touch. Place the dough in a bowl and wrap in clingfilm, then leave in a warm place for 20–30 minutes.

02 Preheat the oven to 190°C/375°F/gas mark 5. Place the rested dough on a lightly floured surface (use cricket flour) and, using a rolling pin, roll the dough out into a large circular shape, about 5mm/¼ inch thick, then spread it out on a large pizza pan or tray.

03 Now let's make the topping. Using a food processor, combine the tomatoes, garlic, salt, pepper and tomato purée until smooth. Spread this mixture evenly over the pizza dough then arrange the pancetta, mozzarella and tomatoes on top.

04 Bake in the hot oven for 20–25 minutes, or until golden brown.

Serve garnished with rocket. This pizza is best eaten straight away. Don't make it too far in advance as the pizza dough will continue to rise if not used at once.

Buffalo worm, tarragon and bacon quiche

For a quiche, you can either grind your chosen insects into flour and use them in the pastry (see page 24) or incorporate them into the soft filling – either works well. In this recipe, I've chosen to keep the buffalo worms in the main mix to ensure that their unique texture and taste is the highlight of the dish.

Serves 2-3

For the pastry

- 175g/6oz/1½ cups plain (all-purpose) flour, plus extra for dusting
- salt, a pinch
- 75g/2¾oz/5 tbsp butter, plus extra for greasing

For the filling

- 200ml/7fl oz/scant 1 cup double (heavy) cream
- 100ml/3½fl oz/scant ½ cup milk
- 5 eggs, beaten
- salt and freshly ground black pepper, a pinch
- 250g/9oz/scant 2¼ cups cheddar
- 50g/1¾oz buffalo worms
- 200g/7oz rashers (slices) of smoked bacon, chopped
- 4 tomatoes, sliced, if you like
- grated 2 tarragon sprigs, chopped
- 1 tbsp smoked paprika

01 To make the pastry, sift the flour together with a pinch of salt in a large bowl. Rub in the butter with your fingertips until you have a soft breadcrumb texture. Add enough cold water to make the crumb mixture come together to form a firm dough, then cover with clingfilm and rest it in the fridge for 30 minutes. Grease a 22cm/8½ inch flan dish generously with butter.

02 Roll out the pastry on a lightly floured surface and use to line the flan dish. Don't cut off the edges of the pastry yet. Chill again for 5 minutes.

03 Preheat the oven to 190°C/375°F/gas mark 5. Remove the pastry case from the fridge. Line the base with parchment paper and fill it with baking beans. Place the case on a baking tray and bake blind for 20 minutes. Remove the beans and parchment and return to the oven for another 5 minutes to cook the base.

04 Meanwhile, whisk the cream, milk, eggs and a pinch of salt and pepper together in a bowl.

05 Lower the temperature of the oven to 160°C/325°F/gas mark 3. Bring the pastry case out of the oven and sprinkle the cheese into the case and add the buffalo worms, bacon, tomatoes, if you like, and the chopped tarragon.

06 Pour the cream and egg mixture into the pastry case, leaving about 5mm/¼ inch from the top free, so it doesn't rise over the edge during cooking. Sprinkle the top with smoked paprika and bake in the hot oven for 30-40 minutes, or until set. Remove from the oven and allow to cool and set further. Before serving, trim the pastry edges to get a clean edge.

Store in the fridge and eat within 2-3 days. If cooled immediately, it freezes well.

Smoked haddock and chive kedgeree with buffalo worm-topped soft-boiled egg

This brightly coloured, aromatic dish is a treat for the senses. In may seem like a minor addition, but the buffalo worm salt adds real savoury spice to the soft-boiled eggs and delicate flakes of haddock. If you double this recipe, you can feast at dinner, then save the leftovers for lunch the next day.

Serves 2-3

- 600ml/1 pint/2½ cups milk
- 600g/1¼lb smoked haddock
- 25g/1oz/2 tbsp butter
- 3 cardamom pods
- 1 cinnamon stick
- ½ tsp ground turmeric
- ½ tsp ground cumin
- ½ tsp curry powder
- 2 bay leaves
- 400g/14oz/2 cups basmati rice
- 600–650ml/20–22fl oz/2½–2¾ cups chicken stock
- 100ml/3½fl oz/½ cup white wine
- salt, to taste
- 5g/⅛oz chives, chopped
- 2 hen's eggs
- a small handful of curly parsley, roughly chopped, to garnish
- buffalo worm salt (see page 26), to top

01 First, heat the milk in a shallow pan over a medium-low heat. Submerge the smoked haddock in the milk and poach for about 6–8 minutes, then remove and allow to cool.

02 Meanwhile, melt the butter in a large pan, add the cardamom, cinnamon, turmeric, cumin, curry powder and bay leaves and stir for 1 minute to infuse the flavours. Add the rice and cook for 2 minutes allowing it to absorb all the flavours.

03 Add the stock, wine and salt to the pan and stir making sure that the rice isn't stuck on the bottom. Cook over a medium heat for about 12–15 minutes, stirring regularly. When ready, the rice should be soft with a bite in the centre of the grain.

04 Finish by flaking the poached fish and chives through the rice.

05 At the same time, have ready a bowl of cold water with ice cubes in it. Bring a pan of salted water to a rolling boil (when water is bubbling) then delicately add the eggs and boil for 6 minutes. Remove and place straight into ice-cold water, then peel.

Serve the rice in a bowl with the soft-boiled egg on top. Garnish with parsley, sprinkle the egg with buffalo worm salt and enjoy.

Cricket and beef mince burritos

Burritos are a brilliant vessel for combining all manner of texture and flavours – it's only fair that insects should be part of the Central American-flavoured party.

Serves 2–3

- 600g/1¼lb beef mince (ground beef)
- ½ white onion, chopped
- 50g/1¾oz crickets
- 1 garlic clove, chopped
- ½ tsp ground cumin
- salt, to taste
- a pinch of black pepper
- 5g/⅛ oz fresh long green chillies, diced
- 400g/14oz can kidney beans
- 200g/7oz beef tomatoes, chopped
- 3 tbsp tomato purée (paste)
- 400g/14oz can chickpeas
- 400g/14oz can chopped tomatoes
- 6 mealworm flour tortillas, warmed (see page 49)
- 200g/7oz/1¾ cups favourite hard cheese of your choice, grated
- 3 spring onions (scallions), chopped
- 50g/1¾oz crispy lettuce, shredded
- 50g/1¾oz red chillies, sliced
- sour cream, to serve

01 Crumble the beef mince into a large, deep pan over a medium-high heat and cook, stirring, until evenly browned. Add the onion and crickets and cook for a few minutes until the onion is translucent.

02 Drain the grease that's come out of the meat from the pan, and season with garlic, cumin, salt and pepper. Stir in the green chillies, kidney beans, beef tomatoes, tomato purée, chickpeas and chopped tomatoes until well blended. Keep over a medium heat until everything is hot throughout.

03 Next, heat the grill. Place a warmed tortilla (see the recipe for mealworm flour tortillas on page 49) on a plate, and spoon a generous 100–120g/3½–4oz/½ cup portion of the cricket and beef mixture into the centre. Top with grated cheese to your liking and briefly melt under the hot grill until golden brown and bubbling.

Remove the tortilla from the grill and top with spring onion, lettuce and chilli, then fold up and eat with a spoonful of sour cream. Repeat this process with the remaining mixture and tortillas. These tortillas are also incredible served with grilled corn on the cob.

Grasshoppers, chestnut mushrooms and pancetta risotto

Nuts of all kinds are often found in risotto recipes, but here we're substituting walnuts for grasshoppers – a slightly more unusual take on the ever-adaptable Italian dish.

Serves 2–3

- 25ml/1fl oz/2 tbsp olive oil
- 1 white onion, finely diced
- 3 garlic cloves, diced
- 50g/1¾oz/3½ tbsp salted butter
- 200g/7oz/scant 1 cup risotto rice
- 800ml/1¾ pints/3½ cups hot vegetable stock
- 40g/1½oz chestnut (cremini) mushrooms, sliced
- 10 grasshoppers, wings and legs removed
- 100ml/3½fl oz/scant ½ cup double (heavy) cream
- 4 rashers (slices) of pancetta or smoked bacon
- 2 tsp chopped chives

01 Heat the oil in a frying pan over a high heat. Once hot, add the onion and garlic and cook for a few minutes until the onion is translucent. Add the butter and allow to melt, then add the risotto rice and fry in the butter for 2–3 minutes to open the grains and allow the flavour to infuse into the rice.

02 Next, add a third of the hot stock and lower the heat to a simmer. Cook the rice, stirring occasionally, and adding a little more stock every time it becomes dry. After about 10–12 minutes when the rice is nearly cooked, add the sliced mushrooms and grasshoppers and continue to cook for another 5 minutes. When the rice is cooked (each grain should be translucent from both ends with a little white still in the middle to give the rice some bite) add the cream and mix through.

03 At the same time while cooking the rice, heat the grill to medium. Grill the pancetta on a grill tray, turning regularly until crispy, then roughly chop into pieces.

Serve in bowls topped with the crispy pancetta and chives.

Mealworm and beef stew

This stew shows off how well mealworms can absorb flavour. As they slow cook, they retain their texture while completely absorbing the flavours of the stew. They're a nutritious and delicious addition to an English classic.

Serves 2–3

- 25ml/1fl oz/2 tbsp rapeseed (canola) oil
- 1 white onion, diced
- 3 garlic cloves, diced
- 400g/14oz stewing steak, ideally beef shin
- 60g/2¼oz mealworms
- 200ml/7fl oz/scant 1 cup red wine
- 2 large carrots, diced
- 1 large potato, peeled and diced
- 1 tsp rosemary sprigs
- 1 litre/1¾ pints/4 cups beef stock
- 1 20 x 20cm/8 x 8 inch sheet of puff pastry
- 1 egg, beaten

01 If you aren't going to use a pressure cooker for this stew then preheat the oven to 200°C/400°F/gas mark 6. Heat the oil in a large, ovenproof saucepan or pressure cooker. Once hot, add the onion and garlic and cook for a few minutes until the onion is translucent. Add the beef and mealworms and fry for another few minutes until the meat is sealed all over and coloured. Add the wine and allow to bubble for a few minutes.

02 Next, add the carrots, potato, rosemary and stock to the pan. Cover with a lid and cook in the hot oven for 1½–2 hours, or until the beef is tender and the sauce thick. Or pressure cook for at least 3 hours or up to 6 hours until the beef is very tender. If you can chop it up with a spoon then it's ready.

03 Now for the topping. Preheat or lower the oven to 180°C/350°F/gas mark 4. Brush the puff pastry with the egg and bake in the hot oven for about 8–10 minutes, or until golden brown and crispy.

When ready, place the stew in bowls and serve topped with puff pastry.

Buffalo worm beef burgers with tomato and lime chutney

Worms and minced beef work well together in many dishes. This is largely because worms, especially buffalo worms, hold their shape very well throughout the cooking process, keeping their texture and flavour. Their unique, earthy taste works in harmony with beef mince here to produce a burger that you will want to make over and over again.

Serves 2

- 700g/1½lb chuck steak, minced
- a pinch each of smoked paprika, ground cumin, cayenne pepper (or replace with Cajun seasoning)
- 3 dashes of Worcestershire sauce
- 2 tsp chopped coriander (cilantro)
- 1 tbsp Dijon mustard
- 1 egg yolk
- 1 tbsp olive oil
- salt and black pepper, to taste
- 100g/3½oz buffalo worms

For tomato and lime chutney

- 200g/7oz tomatoes
- 1 red onion, finely chopped
- 1 red bird's eye (Thai) chilli, sliced
- 30g/1oz/¼ cup sultanas
- 200g/7oz/1 cup dark brown sugar
- zest and juice of 3 limes
- 100ml/3½fl oz/scant ½ cup malt vinegar
- 150ml/5fl oz/⅔ cup red wine
- 1 tsp mixed spice
- 2 garlic cloves, minced
- 2 tsp minced ginger
- 1 cooking apple, peeled, cored and roughly chopped

01 First, get the chutney ready. Chop the tomatoes into rough pieces, then place all the ingredients in a large pan. Lower the heat and cook gently and slowly for about 2 hours, or until the mixture breaks down and becomes syrupy. Allow to cool and then refrigerate.

02 Meanwhile, make the burgers. Place all the burger ingredients in a large bowl and mix together with your hands. It's best to get stuck in at this point, just to make sure that all the ingredients are fully mixed together. Shape the mixture in metal rings. If you don't have any then you can shape them into burger shapes with your hands.

03 Cook the burgers in a large frying pan for about 5 minutes on each side then finish under the grill or in the oven until cooked and piping hot throughout.

Serve the burgers in a toasted bun with beef tomatoes, lettuce and gherkins and a small ramekin of the tomato and lime chutney, mixed leaves and chips on the side.

Baked cricket and mushroom nut loaf

This nut loaf consists of three different layers bound together by an egg mix. The nutty flavour of the crickets acts as an ideal additive to the main mix and results in a prominent flavour that runs through the whole loaf. It's wonderful hot or cold, keeps for 4-5 days in the fridge and freezes well.

Serves 4-5

- 500g/1lb 2oz/3 cups red lentils
- 400g/14oz/2¼ cups brown rice
- 100g/3½oz/1 cup walnuts
- 350g/12oz/3 cups cheddar, grated
- 100g/3½oz/⅔ cup hazelnuts
- 600g/1¼lb carrots, grated
- 150g/5½oz/¾ cup sultanas
- 100g/3½oz/⅔ cup cashews
- 50ml/2fl oz/4 tbsp olive oil
- 2 large onions, finely diced
- 4 garlic cloves, finely chopped
- 20g/¾oz crickets
- 200ml/7fl oz/1 cup white wine
- 70g/2½oz/1½ cups breadcrumbs
- ½ tsp chopped mixed herbs
- 4 large eggs, beaten
- 7 tbsp sweet chilli sauce
- ½ tsp each mild or hot paprika, ground ginger, cinnamon and cumin
- ¼ tsp mixed spice
- 400g/14oz celery, roughly chopped
- 2 thyme sprigs and 1 bay leaf
- 300ml/10fl oz/1¼ cups veg stock
- 200g/7oz chestnut mushrooms
- 200ml/7fl oz/1 cup double (heavy) cream
- salt and black pepper, to taste

01 The easiest way to cook this dish is to first cook the lentils and rice separately (follow the packet instructions). Allow them to cool, then make all four mixes in separate bowls before layering them into an oiled 23cm/9 inch (23cm x 13cm x 8cm) loaf tin. To start, preheat the oven to 190°C/375°F/gas mark 5.

02 For the lentil layer, toast and chop the walnuts then mix them with the cooked lentils and 100g/3½oz/¾ cup of the grated cheddar.

03 For the carrot layer, toast and chop the hazelnuts and mix them with the carrots and sultanas.

04 For the brown rice layer, toast and chop the cashews and mix them with cooked rice and remaining cheddar.

05 For the main mix, heat half the oil in a saucepan over a medium heat, add one of the onions and the garlic and cook for a few minutes until the onion turns translucent. Add the whole crickets then the wine and cook for about 5 minutes. Allow to cool, then mix with the breadcrumbs, chopped herbs, eggs, sweet chilli sauce and spices. This mix should be wetter than the others as it acts as an adhesive.

06 Next, assemble the loaf. Put the lentil layer in the base of the loaf tin. Compress the layer as much as possible with the back of a spoon. Next, add half of the main mix. Then add the carrot layer on top and compress. Add the remaining main mix. Finally, add the brown rice layer and compress. Wrap the top with foil and bake in the oven for 35-45 minutes.

07 For the sauce, heat the remaining oil in a pan over a medium heat. Add the celery, the other onion, thyme and bay leaf and cook for 2-3 minutes. Add the stock and mushrooms and bring to the boil. Cook until it is reduced by a third. Add the cream with salt and pepper to taste.

Serve the nut loaf sliced with the sauce on top.

Cream of celeriac and watercress soup with salted mealworms

The magic in this dish is the salted mealworms. The way they take on flavour is amazing! Drizzle them with plenty of olive oil and salt before roasting – it'll leave you with worms packed full of taste and crunch. A novel alternative to croutons.

Serves 2-3

- 2 tbsp olive oil
- 1 white onion, roughly chopped
- 3 garlic cloves, peeled
- 50g/1¾oz/3½ tbsp butter
- 1 celeriac, peeled and chopped into chunks
- 30g/1oz mealworms
- a pinch of coarse salt
- 700ml/1½ pints/3 cups vegetable stock
- 200ml/7fl oz/scant 1 cup double (heavy) cream
- 50g/1¾oz watercress
- salt and ground white pepper, to taste

01 Preheat the oven to 180°C/350°F/gas mark 4. Heat a splash of oil in a large deep pan over a medium heat. Add the onion and garlic and cook for a few minutes until the onion has turned translucent. Add the butter then once it has melted add the celeriac and fry for a few minutes until it begins to colour.

02 Meanwhile, lightly coat the mealworms with the remaining olive oil and sprinkle with coarse salt. Spread the mealworms over a baking tray in a single layer and roast in the hot oven for about 10 minutes, or until they are crispy.

03 Next, add the stock to the pan and lower the heat to a simmer. Simmer the vegetables for about 15 minutes until soft. Add the cream and watercress, then take off the heat and, using a hand-held blender, blitz until smooth. Check the seasoning and adjust to taste.

Serve in individual bowls with a little watercress on top and some crispy salted mealworms. This is great with a slice of toasted mealworm bread, which you can find on page 56.

Sauces, dips, dressings and pastes

Grasshopper, Thai basil and cashew nut dressing

This dressing is a fine accompaniment to salads. It's particularly lovely as a dressing for spicy salads as the natural creaminess of the cashew nuts cuts nicely through the intensity of the chillies. Thai basil can be purchased in any good Asian supermarket and its natural aniseed flavour is a perfect partner to the nutty taste of the grasshoppers. But don't worry if you haven't the time to hunt for it, normal basil will do.

Makes about 500ml/17fl oz/2 cups

- 5g/¹⁄₈oz grasshoppers, legs and wings removed
- 100ml/3½fl oz/scant ½ cup light soy sauce
- 50g/1¾oz/¹⁄₃ cup toasted cashews
- 30g/1oz Thai basil leaves (ordinary basil works too)
- 5g/¹⁄₈oz garlic, peeled
- 450ml/15fl oz/scant 2 cups olive oil
- a little crushed black pepper

01 In a bowl, soak the grasshoppers in the soy sauce for 1 hour, then pass them through a sieve to remove any excess soy.

02 To make the dressing, place all the ingredients in a food processor, including the grasshoppers, and blitz until smooth. There's no need to add any salt as the soy from the grasshoppers is enough. Season to taste with crushed black pepper.

This dressing can be refrigerated for up to 7 days, but is best eaten fresh within a few days after making. If it's left for too long out of the fridge the basil will turn brown making the dressing much less desirable.

Spiced grasshopper, butter bean and lime hummus

For a healthy hummus that packs a punch, try this blended mix of grasshoppers, butter beans and chillies. Couple with mealworm flour tortilla chips (on page 49) for a double dose of insect goodness.

Serves 3

- 400g/14oz canned butter (lima beans)
- 15g/½oz/generous ¼ cup ground grasshopper (see page 24)
- 2 long green chillies, roughly chopped
- 3 garlic cloves, peeled
- salt, a pinch
- juice of ½ lime
- a few coriander (cilantro) leaves, finely chopped, to garnish

01 Whizz all the ingredients (except the coriander) in a food processor until thick. Transfer to a bowl.

Sprinkle with chopped coriander leaves to serve.

Roasted red pepper, anchovy and buffalo worm pesto

This is a simple sauce with a complex flavour. Buffalo worms can sometimes have quite a shrimp-like taste, which works in oily fish dishes. If you're not a fan of anchovies, substitute them with any other oily fish, such as mackerel, herring or sardines.

Serves 2

- 2 red (bell) peppers, deseeded, cored and roughly chopped
- 1 garlic clove, diced
- 50g/1¾oz buffalo worms
- 150ml/5fl oz/²⁄₃ cup olive oil
- 470g/17oz can anchovies in oil, drained
- salt and freshly ground black pepper, to taste

01 Preheat the oven to 180°C/350°F/gas mark 4. Coat the peppers, garlic and worms in a little of the oil then spread them out on a non-stick baking tray. Roast in the hot oven for 15 minutes until they begin to colour and all the flavours are released.

02 Next, put the roasted mixture into a food processor with the anchovies and the rest of the oil, then season with salt and pepper and whizz to combine.

This pesto will keep in the fridge for up to a week. It's amazing used as a dressing for salads or mixed with pasta as a sauce.

Buffalo worm salt guacamole

Perhaps Mexico's most famous culinary export, guacamole has found its way into homes all over the world. And with good reason. The subtle creaminess of avocado means the flavour combinations are endless – in this case, that means pairing it with buffalo worm salt, cayenne pepper and basil. It's wonderful served alongside the cricket and beef burritos on page 102, and the mealworm flour tortilla chips on page 49.

Serves 3

- 15g/½ oz buffalo worms
- 1 tsp salt
- 1 large beef tomato, chopped
- 3 ripe avocados, stoned and peeled
- 20g/¾oz coriander (cilantro) leaves
- 1 small red onion, diced
- juice of ½ lime
- 20g/¾oz basil leaves
- 1 large green chilli, deseeded and finely chopped
- tortilla chips, to serve (see page 49)

01 First, dry-roast the buffalo worms in a pan over a medium heat for a few minutes. They'll turn a golden brown colour, at which point turn off the heat. Put the salt and buffalo worms in a mortar and use the pestle to pound them to make buffalo worm salt. Set aside.

02 Next, put the rest of the ingredients into a food processor and pulse to blend them together. Don't blend them too much as it's good for it to be a bit chunky.

Put the guacamole in a bowl, top with the buffalo worm salt and serve with tortilla chips to dip (see page 49).

If it's not eaten straight away then put the avocado stone into the guacamole, squeeze a bit of lime over the top, wrap in clingfilm and refrigerate. This will prevent the mixture turning brown. For best results eat immediately after making, otherwise consume within 24 hours.

Buffalo worm green curry paste

Fermented shrimp are common in many Thai curry pastes, but here I have used buffalo worms instead. They add a depth of flavour that really enhances the spicy paste. Many of the ingredients for this paste can be found in good supermarkets; however kra chi (wild ginger), lemongrass and galangal may need to be sourced from an Asian supermarket.

Makes 300g/10½oz paste

- 25g/1oz white peppercorns
- 25g/1oz whole coriander (cilantro) seeds
- 2 tsp cumin seeds
- 20g/¾oz piece galangal, peeled and finely chopped
- 50g/1¾oz lemongrass, outer layer and stems removed, then finely chopped
- 10g/⅓oz kaffir lime leaves, finely shredded
- 5g/⅛oz coriander (cilantro) root (if available, though it works without)
- 6 green bird's eye (Thai) chillies, roughly chopped
- 2 long green chillies, deseeded and roughly chopped
- 30g/1oz garlic, peeled
- 10g/⅓oz piece wild ginger (kra chi is available in good Asian grocery stores, otherwise use normal ginger), peeled and chopped
- 50g/1¾oz banana shallots, finely diced
- 60g/2¼oz buffalo worms, puréed (see page 25)

01 The easiest way to go about making a curry paste is to make sure you have a large granite mortar and pestle. Pastes are combined through brute force so the heavier the better. Although the process is very simple, it can be time consuming, but the best way is to pound up each ingredient one by one, the toughest first, and then combine them all in the mortar at the end. Once all the ingredients are prepared correctly it's just between you and the pestle.

02 First, toast the white peppercorns, coriander seeds and cumin seeds in a dry frying pan for a few minutes, shaking the pan now and again to make sure they don't burn, then grind them to a powder in a spice grinder or mortar and pestle.

03 Next, pound all the fresh ingredients, one by one in the mortar and pestle, in this order: galangal, lemongrass, kaffir lime leaves, coriander root, chillies, garlic, ginger and shallots, then add the ground spices and worm purée and mix them all together.

This curry paste is delicious cooked with coconut cream and served with prawns. The shrimpy, nutty buffalo worms add a perfect base flavour. The paste can be kept in an airtight container in the fridge for 3-4 weeks. Don't use if it has gone brown.

Buffalo worm red curry paste

This curry paste uses slightly fewer ingredients than the green paste on the previous page, but it still has loads of flavour. Combine with coconut cream, chicken, vegetables and fresh Thai basil for a true taste of South East Asia.

Makes 600g/1¼lb paste

- 150g/5½oz dried long red chillies
- 2 tbsp white peppercorns
- 2 tbsp whole coriander (cilantro) seeds
- 4 tsp cumin seeds
- 20g/¾oz piece galangal, peeled and diced
- 50g/1¾oz lemongrass, outer layer and stems removed, then finely chopped
- 100g/3½oz garlic, peeled
- 150g/5½oz banana shallots, finely diced
- 30g/1oz coriander (cilantro) root, if you can find it (it works without)
- 100g/3½oz buffalo worms, puréed (see page 25)

01 The easiest way to go about making a curry paste is to make sure you have a large granite mortar and pestle. Pastes are combined through brute force so the heavier the better. Although the process is very simple, it can be time consuming, but the best way is to pound up each ingredient one by one, the toughest first, and then combine them all in the mortar at the end. Once all ingredients are prepared correctly it's just between you and the pestle.

02 First, soak the dried chillies in a bowl of warm water for 30 minutes. Meanwhile, toast the white peppercorns, coriander seeds and cumin seeds in a dry frying pan for a few minutes, shaking the pan now and again to make sure they don't burn, then grind them to a powder in a spice grinder or mortar and pestle.

04 Once the dried chillies are soft, remove from the water and slice them lengthways in half, then put them back into the water to remove all the seeds. Drain.

05 Next, pound all the fresh ingredients, one by one in the mortar and pestle, in this order: dried chillies, galangal, lemongrass, garlic, shallots and coriander root, then add the ground spices and worm purée and mix them all together.

This is great cooked with coconut cream, chicken, Thai basil and vegetables. The paste can be kept in an airtight container in the fridge for 3–4 weeks. Don't use if it has gone brown.

Mealworm satay sauce

The inclusion of mealworms in this satay sauce creates a unique flavour you're unlikely to have tasted before. They add earthy, shrimp-like tones that work very well with grilled chicken skewers. Red curry paste can be purchased ready made from most supermarkets, but you can also make it from scratch by following my recipe on page 129.

Serves 2

- 3 tbsp vegetable oil
- 40g/1½oz red curry paste
- 1 tbsp mild curry powder
- 20g/¾oz/2 tbsp palm sugar or soft brown sugar
- 300ml/10fl oz/1¼ cups coconut cream
- 100ml/3½fl oz/scant ½ cup vegetable stock
- 60g/2¼oz/scant ½ cup peanuts, crushed using a mincer/food processor
- 40g/1½oz mealworms, crushed (in a mortar and pestle)
- 3 tbsp fish sauce

01 First, heat the oil in a wok over a medium heat, then add the red curry paste and stir-fry, adding a little more oil if needed for 1 minute, or until the paste begins to smell fragrant (it will also split a little making it almost look like red scrambled eggs). At this point add the curry powder and palm sugar and continue to stir, moving the paste constantly. The sugar will melt and begin to caramelise, darkening the paste.

02 Next, add the coconut cream and stock and bring the mixture to a simmer. Add the crushed peanuts and mealworms and stir well. The peanuts act as a thickening agent, bringing the ingredients together to create a thick, creamy, rich sauce.

03 Finally, finish the seasoning with the fish sauce. Do bear in mind that the strength of the ingredients can be inconsistent, so always taste to check your sauce – you may need to adjust the seasoning to your own liking. The key to success when making a satay is the balance in seasoning; it should be salty and sour with a sweet edge.

This is ideal served with steamed rice and eaten as soon as it's ready. Coconut cream doesn't hold very well, so for the tastiest results eat straight away.

Spiced buffalo worm barbecue sauce

The buffalo worms in this recipe add a fishy flavour not usually found in barbecue sauces, but trust me, this one's a real game changer. The best way to use barbecue sauce is to baste it on to meat as you grill it: that way the sugar and salt cooks into the meat. But of course it works just as well as a dip. Whichever way you choose to eat it, it's guaranteed to please.

Makes roughly 500g/1lb 2oz

- 1 tbsp olive oil
- 1 red onion, finely chopped
- 3 garlic cloves, finely chopped
- 2 long red chillies, finely chopped and deseeded if you don't want it too spicy
- 85g/3oz/scant ½ cup soft brown sugar
- 2 tbsp red wine vinegar
- 3 tbsp malt vinegar
- 400g/14oz can chopped tomatoes
- 1 tsp ground pink peppercorns
- 4 tbsp ground buffalo worms
- 2 tbsp Worcestershire sauce
- 1 tbsp ketjap manis (Indonesian sweet soy sauce)
- 1 tbsp fish sauce
- 1 tbsp tomato purée (paste)
- salt, a pinch

01 Heat the oil in a saucepan over a gentle heat, then add the onion, garlic and chillies and cook for 4–5 minutes until softened.
02 Next, add the sugar and both vinegars to the pan and cook for 1 minute to darken the sugar.
03 Add all the remaining ingredients, season and mix well. Bring to the boil, then lower the heat and simmer for 20–30 minutes, or until thickened. For a smooth sauce, simply whizz the mixture in a food processor or with a hand-held blender for a few seconds.

Due to the salt and sugar content in this sauce it keeps well in an airtight container in the fridge for 2–3 weeks.

Cherry tomato, mascarpone and grasshopper pasta sauce

Packed full of fresh basil leaves, this creamy sauce is wonderful poured over freshly cooked pasta and topped with cheese.

Serves 2-3

- 25ml/1fl oz/2 tbsp rapeseed (canola) oil
- 15 grasshoppers
- 2 garlic cloves, diced
- 200g/7oz cherry tomatoes
- 200g/7oz canned chopped tomatoes
- 1 tbsp tomato purée (paste)
- 150g/5½oz/²/₃ cup mascarpone cheese
- 200ml/7fl oz/scant 1 cup double (heavy) cream
- salt and freshly ground black pepper, to taste

01 In a large frying pan, heat the oil over a high heat. Once hot, add the grasshoppers, garlic and fresh tomatoes, canned tomatoes and tomato purée and fry for about 5 minutes until the garlic has browned and the tomatoes are sizzling.

02 Next, add this mixture to a food processor with the rest of the ingredients and whizz until smooth.

03 Pour the sauce into a pan over a low heat and bring back to a simmer before serving.

Desserts

Mum's fat-free mealworm malt loaf

This is based on a very easy recipe that has been handed down through my family, and it's the perfect treat at tea time. Soaking the fruit overnight in tea (without milk) means the loaf keeps that all-important moisture, and its wonderfully rich taste belies the fact that it's fat free. Of course, this recipe has been slightly adapted for the purposes of this book... I don't recall my grandma adding mealworm flour. But I'm sure she would have loved it!

Makes 1 sharing-sized malt loaf

- 250g/9oz/1½ cups mixed dried fruit (sultanas/golden raisins and juicy raisins are good as well as a few cranberries)
- 100g/3½oz/½ cup soft brown sugar, plus extra for sprinkling
- 225ml/8fl oz/1 cup hot, well-stewed black tea
- ¼ tsp ground cinnamon
- ¼ tsp mixed spice
- salt, a pinch
- 1 large egg, beaten
- 175g/6oz/scant 1½ cups self-raising flour
- 80g/3oz/scant ½ cup mealworm flour (see page 24)

01 Put the dried fruit and sugar into a large bowl. Gently pour in the hot tea and mix in thoroughly. Cover with clingfilm and leave for a few hours. The longer you leave it the plumper the fruit becomes. Overnight gets the best results.

02 When you're ready, preheat the oven to 160°C/325°F/gas mark 3 and line a 500g/1lb 2oz loaf tin with parchment paper. Stir the spices, salt and beaten egg into the soaked fruit and tea mixture with a wooden spoon, then add the self-raising flour and mealworm flour.

03 Spoon the mixture into the lined tin, spreading it evenly in the tin. Sprinkle a little sugar on top if you fancy an extra treat, and bake in the hot oven for 45 minutes–1 hour. Test that it's cooked through by inserting the point of a knife or skewer in the centre and checking it comes out clean. Allow to cool on a wire rack before slicing.

For best results store the malt loaf wrapped in clingfilm in the fridge and eat within 3–4 days after making. It's great with a cup of tea and a thin spreading of butter.

Cricket flour scones with fresh fruit and clotted cream

A little bit of cricket flour makes these scones extra special, and I've experimented a lot to get these just right (which is why the recipe doesn't stick to the advised ratio of 1 part insect flour to 2 parts traditional flour). I've heard people describe cricket flour as being similar to cocoa powder and I always thought it was a load of rubbish, but just wait until you make these...

Makes about 8 scones

- 20g/¾oz/scant ¼ cup cricket flour (see page 24)
- 230g/8½oz/2 cups self-raising flour, plus extra for dusting
- 40g/1½oz/3 tbsp unsalted butter, at room temperature
- 1½ tbsp caster (superfine) sugar
- salt, a pinch
- 110ml/3½fl oz/scant ½ cup milk
- a little icing (confectioners') sugar, for dusting
- butter, jam, clotted cream and a selection of your favourite fruit, to serve

01 Sift both flours together. In a large bowl, using your fingertips, rub the butter into the sifted flour. Add the sugar followed by the salt, then mix in the milk a little bit at a time until it has all been added. It is best to use a palette knife to do this as the mixture becomes temporarily sticky.

02 Next, knead the mixture to a soft dough on a clean, lightly floured surface with your hands. Use a rolling pin to lightly roll out the dough to about 3cm/1¼ inches thick (the thickness is important as the scones will not rise if the dough is too thin).

03 Use a circular pastry cutter to cut out as many rounds as you can from the dough. When you have cut as many as you can, re-knead the remaining dough back together and repeat the process. You should be able to get a few extra rounds.

04 Place the scones on a baking sheet, dust each one with icing sugar and bake on the top shelf of the hot oven for 12–15 minutes until they have risen and turned a golden brown colour.

05 Transfer them to a wire rack and allow to cool.

Serve the scones with butter, jam and clotted cream. They taste great with the sweet banana and grasshopper jam recipe on page 161. Store the scones in an airtight container in a cool, dry place. For best results eat within a few days of making.

Grilled bananas with ants, sesame, tamarind and palm sugar caramel

This is a quick and simple recipe that uses the natural citrussy flavour of ants to great effect. Alongside the tamarind, they strike a balance with the sweet stickiness of the caramel and banana, while the salt brings it all together. For best results grill the banana over a barbecue (although a grill pan will do).

Serves 2

- heaped ½ tsp sesame seeds
- 2 bananas, unpeeled
- 100ml /3½fl oz/scant ½ cup tamarind water (from Asian grocery stores)
- 50g/1¾oz/¼ cup palm sugar, or soft brown sugar will do too
- 1 tsp wood ants (*Formica rufa*), these are best sourced from an experienced forager and should be frozen as soon as they're collected. Defrost and use without further preparation

01 First, toast the sesame seeds. Preheat the oven to 180°C/350°F/gas mark 4. Spread the sesame seeds out on a baking sheet and toast them in the hot oven for 15-20 minutes, stirring regularly to make sure that they don't burn. Take them out of the oven as soon as they turn a light golden brown colour and allow to cool.

02 Heat a stovetop grill pan or barbecue over a high heat. Slice the bananas lengthways and place on the hot grill pan or barbecue, skin-side up. Grill for 2-3 minutes until the bananas turn golden brown.

03 At the same time, bring the tamarind water and palm sugar to the boil in a saucepan and heat to 115°C/239°F, or until it begins to thicken, then take off the heat.

Place the grilled bananas on a plate, cover with the palm sugar and tamarind caramel then sprinkle with the toasted sesame seeds and the ants. This dish should taste sweet and sour, and serving it with vanilla ice cream is inspired.

Cricket flour milk chocolate and raspberry brownie

These are perfect as a dessert, a present for a friend or simply a treat for yourself. Follow the simple instructions for making your own cricket flour on page 24.

Makes 12 large brownies

- 225g/8oz/1 cup unsalted butter, plus extra for greasing
- 450g/1lb/2¼ cups caster (superfine) sugar
- 140g/5oz milk chocolate, broken into pieces
- 50g/1¾oz/scant ½ cup fresh raspberries, plus an extra handful to decorate
- 5 eggs
- 100g/3½oz/scant 1 cup plain (all-purpose) flour
- 50g/1¾oz/scant ½ cup cricket flour (see page 24)
- 50g/1¾oz/½ cup (unsweetened) cocoa powder

01 Preheat the oven to 190°C/375°F/gas mark 5 and line a deep baking tray or brownie tin with parchment paper. Rub the sides of the lined tray or tin with a little butter. This makes it easier to remove the brownie after it has been cooked.

02 Gently melt the butter and sugar together in a large saucepan until the ingredients combine into a pourable liquid. Take off the heat and, using a whisk, whisk in the rest of the ingredients, whisking well. The gentle heat of the melted butter and sugar will melt the chocolate to leave you with a brown-coloured, thick brownie mix.

03 Pour the mixture into the baking tray and bake in the hot oven for 30-40 minutes until cooked. To check, stick the point of a knife or skewer in the centre of the brownie and remove: the brownie is ready when the knife or skewer comes back out clean, with no mix on it.

04 Allow to cool in the tray, then carefully turn out and cut into 12 large squares.

These brownies are delightful to eat warm and gooey straight from the oven, decorated with raspberries and served with ice cream or double cream. If left to cool they can then be cut into portions and will keep for 3-4 days in the fridge. They also freeze well.

White chocolate, orange and grasshopper mousse

This fluffy chocolate mousse is just the ticket if you're after a light (yet indulgent) dessert after a big meal. Fresh orange zest and toasted grasshoppers give this pud a delicious edge that make it extra moreish.

Makes 4 portions

- 250ml/9fl oz/generous 1 cup double (heavy) cream
- 100g/3½oz white chocolate, roughly chopped, plus extra for dusting
- finely grated zest of 1 orange, plus extra for garnish
- 2 egg whites
- 25g/1oz/2 tbsp caster (superfine) sugar
- 8 grasshoppers, dry-roasted in a pan over a low heat until golden brown
- cocoa powder, for dusting

01 Heat the cream in a heatproof bowl set over a pan of gently simmering water. Make sure the bottom of the bowl doesn't touch the water. Add the white chocolate and orange zest and stir regularly until the chocolate has melted.

02 Once the chocolate has melted, wrap the bowl in clingfilm and place in the fridge for about 2 hours, or until cold.

03 Whisk the egg whites in a grease-free bowl with an electric whisk until they are stiff and hold their shape. Add the sugar and whisk until stiff again.

04 Fold the egg whites into the cold chocolate cream making sure not to knock all the whipped air out of the egg whites, then pour the mixture into 150ml/5fl oz/⅔ cup ramekins. Place 2 toasted grasshoppers on top to decorate.

These look great dusted with a little cocoa powder, finely grated orange zest and grated white chocolate. If not consumed straight away keep in the fridge and eat within 3 days.

Buffalo worm, peanut and vanilla praline

This candy is fantastic on its own as a quick treat but can also be enjoyed with ice cream and other desserts. Praline is best stored in between baking paper and kept in a container as it is fragile and sticky; it can also be frozen for a later date. If you have a nut allergy, this recipe works well without the peanuts.

Serves 2–3

- 200g/7oz/1 cup caster (superfine) sugar
- 100ml/3½fl oz/scant ½ cup water
- ½ vanilla pod (bean) or 1 tbsp vanilla extract
- 10g/⅓oz buffalo worms
- 40g/1½oz/¼ cup peanuts, crushed or roughly chopped

01 First, line an oven tray with parchment paper. Melt the sugar and water in a saucepan over a medium heat, stirring regularly until the sugar has dissolved.

02 Split the vanilla pod in half lengthways and scrape the seeds out with the back of your knife and add these to the pan. Continue to heat until the sugar begins to caramelise, about 4–5 minutes. It's ready when it turns toffee-brown and thickens. Keep your eyes on the bubbling mixture as it will turn black and be inedible if it's overcooked. I've seen many a chef burn their praline! Trust me, it's not very tasty.

03 Take off the heat and quickly stir in the buffalo worms and peanuts. Pour this straight on to the tray and spread out as thinly as possible using the back of a wooden spoon. Allow to cool in the fridge. The praline should set after 30 minutes.

04 Bash it with a rolling pin to break into bite-sized pieces.

Cricket flour cinnamon cookies

*These cookies are destined for cosy evenings with a cup of tea or hot chocolate in hand –
the warm scent of cinnamon as they bake will have you counting down the seconds until
you can take them out the oven. Let them sit for a few minutes though, then tuck in.
The maple syrup should give them that all-important chewy centre.*

Makes about 15 cookies

- 120g/4oz/½ cup unsalted butter, plus extra for greasing
- 50g/1¾ oz/¼ cup light muscovado sugar
- 80g/3oz/scant ½ cup caster (superfine) sugar
- 1 medium egg
- ½ tsp ground cinnamon
- 20g/¾oz/1 tbsp maple syrup
- 70g/2½oz/½ cup cricket flour (see page 24), sifted
- 100g/3½oz/scant 1 cup plain (all- purpose) flour, sifted
- ½ tsp baking powder
- 50g/1¾oz/⅓ cup raisins

01 First, preheat the oven to 190°C/375°F/gas mark 5 and line a baking tray with parchment paper, then lightly grease the paper with butter.

02 Melt the butter in a pan over a low heat then take off the heat and stir in the muscovado and caster sugars.

03 In a separate bowl, beat the egg and cinnamon together, then stir into the butter and sugar mix with the maple syrup. Add the flours and baking powder to the bowl and stir together to combine. Finally, add the raisins.

04 Spoon circles of the mixture onto the prepared tray, making sure they are spaced apart, or else they will spread during cooking and stick together.

05 Bake in the hot oven for about 10–12 minutes, or until the cookies are golden brown. Allow to cool before eating.

The cookies are great served with a glass of ice-cold milk with a sprinkling of grated chocolate on the top. They can be kept in an airtight container for 2-3 days, if they last that long.

Grasshopper condensed milk ice cream

Condensed milk ice cream is a truly addictive dessert. I like to top it with toasted grasshoppers for an added nutty crunch and a sprig of mint for a burst of freshness. You can also team it with the buffalo worm, peanut and vanilla praline (see page 149).

Makes about 750g/1lb 10oz

- 7 egg yolks
- 50g/1¾oz/¼ cup caster (superfine) sugar
- salt, a pinch
- 250g/9oz/generous 1 cup canned condensed milk
- 500ml/17fl oz/2 cups thick double (heavy) cream
- 10 roasted and ground grasshoppers
- mint leaves, to decorate

01 Using an electric whisk, whisk the egg yolks, sugar and a pinch of salt together in a large heatproof bowl until thick and full of air.

02 Heat the condensed milk in a heatproof bowl set over a pan of gently simmering water. Make sure the bottom of the bowl doesn't touch the water. Once hot, slowly whisk the hot condensed milk into the egg and sugar mix. Keep whisking and only add a small amount of the milk at a time otherwise the eggs will scramble.

03 Once combined pour the mixture back into the condensed milk bowl and set again over a pan of gently simmering water. Stir regularly until the mixture thickens to a custard consistency then take off the heat and allow to cool in the fridge.

04 Whip the cream in a large bowl with an electric whisk to soft peaks (so you can draw a line in it and it holds for a few seconds). Fold the whipped cream into the cooled condensed milk mixture, making sure that both mixtures are cold. Try to be very careful not to knock the air out of it while mixing.

05 Finish by sprinkling the grasshoppers over the mixture then put into a freezerproof container and freeze overnight before serving. If you like, stir the mixture once or twice while it's freezing as this helps in the freezing process.

Serve the ice cream, decorated with mint leaves and some of the buffalo worm, peanut and vanilla praline (see page 149) on the side.

Insect chimp stick

This is another popular dish from the Grub pop-up events. A chopstick is coated in palm sugar and tamarind caramel and then dipped in a mixture of crispy shallots, peanuts, coconuts and insects. The result is indulgently sweet and gooey. We've called it a chimp stick as it's inspired by apes who use twigs dipped in sticky tree sap to collect their tasty and nutritious insect dinner.

Makes 5 sticks

- 1 litre/1¾ pints/4 cups vegetable oil, for deep-frying
- 30g/1oz banana shallots, finely sliced
- 10g/⅓oz lemongrass, outer layer and stalk removed, finely sliced
- 10g/⅓oz kaffir lime leaves, stems removed
- 30g/1oz crickets
- 30g/1oz buffalo worms
- 30g/1oz mealworms
- 2 tsp water
- 4 tsp fish sauce
- 150g/5½oz/¾ cup palm sugar
- 200g/7oz/1⅓ cups toasted peanuts, roughly broken
- 200g/7oz/2¼ cups desiccated (dry unsweetened) coconut, toasted
- 5 chopsticks

01 Heat the oil in a large deep saucepan to 180°C/350°F, or until a cube of bread browns in 30 seconds. Most of the ingredients are going to be fried and they all cook at different rates, so first fry the shallots as they take the longest. Carefully add them to the oil and deep-fry for about 6-7 minutes, or until golden brown, then remove with a slotted spoon and drain on kitchen paper.

02 Next, deep-fry the lemongrass, then the kaffir lime leaves. When these are all fried, move on to the insects. Once again these all brown and crisp at different rates so fry and drain them all separately. Once everything has been fried and drained on kitchen paper mix it all together on a large baking tray lined with kitchen paper.

03 Heat the water, fish sauce and palm sugar in a large pan over a high heat, stirring constantly. You are making a caramel, so the mixture needs to bubble, however, make sure it doesn't catch or it will be ruined. Once the mixture has reached 115°C/239°F it's ready.

04 Add the peanuts and coconut to the deep-fried mixture then remove the kitchen paper from underneath them and discard.

05 One at a time, coat 5 chopsticks in the caramel, leaving enough space for you to hold the stick while eating it. Be really careful not to burn yourself as the caramel is hot.

06 Once the caramel is on, dunk it in the fried mixture, pushing the mix on to the stick to help it stick to the caramel. Finally, set aside to let the mixture set onto the caramel. Repeat until all the mixture is used up.

If you don't eat these straight away, the caramel can set very hard and become brittle. If this happens just place in an oven preheated to 180°C/350°F/gas mark 4 for 1 minute, then serve.

Cricket, raisin and nut flapjack

These are a top treat to have stored in your cupboard for when you need a quick energy fix. The nuts and crickets lift the deep sweetness of the black treacle and combine to create a terrific afternoon pick-me-up.

Makes 12 portions

- 150g/5½oz/scant ¾ cup unsalted butter, plus extra for greasing
- 125g/4oz/scant ⅔ cup soft brown sugar
- 2 tbsp black treacle (blackstrap molasses)
- 55g/2oz/⅓ cup mixed pistachios and hazelnuts, crushed
- 75g/2¾oz crickets
- 200g/7oz/2⅓ cups jumbo porridge (rolled) oats
- salt, a pinch

01 First, preheat the oven to 150°C/300°F/gas mark 2 and grease a shallow rectangular baking tin with butter. Melt the butter, sugar and black treacle together in a medium pan over a medium heat until it is melted and completely combined.

02 Take the pan off the heat and mix in the nuts, crickets, porridge oats and salt until it is all combined.

03 Pour the mixture into the tin and bake in the hot oven for 25–30 minutes until golden brown. Take out of the oven and allow to cool. The mixture should become harder, but not brittle. Turn out of the tin and chop into 12 pieces and enjoy.

Store in an airtight container and eat within 7 days.

Thickened coconut cream fruit salad with sesame seeds and ants

Ants have a naturally sour burst when bitten into, making them an ideal ingredient to add to a fruit salad. Drizzled in a salted coconut cream sauce, this dessert is wonderful after a heavy meal.

Serves 2-3

- 20g/¾oz/⅛ cup blackberries
- 20g/¾oz/scant ¼ cup raspberries
- 20g/¾oz/⅛ cup strawberries
- 20g/¾oz mango, peeled and stoned
- ½ pomegranate, seeds removed
- 1-2 kiwi fruits, peeled, halved and sliced into half moons
- 200ml/7fl oz/scant 1 cup coconut cream
- 30g/1oz/generous ⅛ cup rice flour
- 1 tsp caster (superfine) sugar
- scant 2 tsp salt
- 10g/⅓oz wood ants (*Formica rufa*): these are best sourced from an experienced forager and should be frozen as soon as they're collected. Defrost and use without further preparation

01 Arrange the fruit however you would like in a bowl. This recipe is just a selection of my favourites, so you're in charge and include as much fruit as you would like.

02 To thicken the coconut cream, bring it to a simmer in a pan over a low heat. In a small heatproof bowl, make a paste out of the rice flour using a little bit of the coconut cream. Whisk this paste briefly to make sure there are no lumps then add it to the rest of the coconut cream along with the caster sugar and salt. Simmer for a minute or so until the mixture has thickened.

The fruit salad is heavenly with the warm sauce drizzled over the top and then the ants sprinkled over. However, if you can wait, allow the sauce to cool and then serve.

Sweet banana and grasshopper jam

No matter how many different foods I come across, there is one that will always hold a special place in my heart – jam! Banana in jam is a recent discovery and it's scrumptious. This is great with grasshoppers, as when roasted they are similar in taste to walnuts. Spread generously over toast (see page 56) or cricket flour scones (see page 140).

Makes a 1kg/2¼lb jar of jam

- 800g/1¾lb bananas, peeled and roughly chopped
- juice of 2 limes
- 110ml /3½fl oz/scant ½ cup water
- 450g/1lb/2¼ cups jam sugar (with added pectin)
- 10 grasshoppers, roasted and roughly chopped

01 To start, cover the chopped bananas in the lime juice. This will preserve the colour of the banana so that the jam remains yellow, rather than turns brown.

02 Heat the water and sugar in a medium pan over a medium heat, then take off the heat and wrap the pan in foil. Leave for 1 minute then uncover. The steam produced cleans all the excess sugar off the sides of the pan, making sure it does not burn.

03 Once the sugar has melted, add the grasshoppers and bananas with the lime juice and continue to cook over a medium heat, stirring regularly until it reaches 120°C/248°F on a sugar thermometer, or until it's thick. Don't allow the mixture to stick to the pan.

04 Carefully pour the jam into a sterilised jar and allow to cool before sealing with a lid and storing in the fridge for up to 2-3 months.

Cricket, apple and cinnamon bread and butter pudding with butterscotch sauce

Soaking crickets in orange juice with dried fruit is a really unusual way to use them. The custard in this recipe binds all the layers of bread and fruit together once it's baked, so make sure you fill all the gaps before baking. A shot of rum in the butterscotch gives it an adult twist.

Serves 3-4

- 75g/2¾oz/scant ½ cup sultanas
- 15g/½oz crickets
- 50ml/1¾fl oz/scant ¼ cup orange juice
- 125g/4oz/½ cup salted butter, plus extra for greasing
- 1 loaf of sliced bread
- 3 apples, peeled, cored and sliced
- 50g/1¾oz/scant ¼ cup marmalade

For the custard

- 300ml/10fl oz/1¼ cups double (heavy) cream
- 300ml/10fl oz/1¼ cups milk
- 1 vanilla pod (bean)
- 1 cinnamon stick
- 120g/4oz/generous ½ cup caster (superfine) sugar
- 1 tsp ground cinnamon
- 8 egg yolks

For the butterscotch sauce

- 60g/2¼oz/¼ cup butter
- 150g/5½oz/¾ cup brown sugar
- 150ml/5fl oz/⅔ cup double (heavy) cream
- 1 tbsp golden (light corn) syrup

01 First, soak the sultanas and crickets in separate bowls of boiling water and 25ml/1fl oz/2 tablespoons orange juice for at least 1 hour or overnight for best results, then drain and set aside.

02 When ready to make the dish, preheat the oven to 180°C/350°F/ gas mark 4 and grease a 500g/1lb 2oz loaf tin with butter.

03 Start with the custard. Gently simmer the cream, milk and vanilla pod, split lengthways in half, together in a large pan over a medium heat (don't let it boil).

04 Meanwhile, mix the sugar with the cinnamon in a heatproof bowl, then add the egg yolks and whisk together. Pour the hot cream and milk on to the yolks, while stirring constantly to stop the eggs scrambling, then return to the pan and heat again over a medium heat, stirring regularly until it thickens.

05 Butter the bread on both sides and remove the crusts, then arrange a layer of the bread in the bottom of the tin. Sprinkle over the soaked sultanas, sliced apple and soaked crickets. Pour over enough of the custard to cover then repeat until the pudding is about 1cm/½ inch short of the top of the tin. The top layer is just bread: put it on neatly. Pour over the rest of the custard and make sure it is soaked in properly, filling all the gaps. Bake in the hot oven for 40-45 minutes until golden brown. Take out of the oven and brush the marmalade over the top to glaze.

06 Finally, make the butterscotch sauce. Melt the butter in a small pan over a low heat. Stir in the sugar, cream and syrup. When the sugar has dissolved, bring the mixture to the boil, then take off the heat.

Serve hot alongside the bread and butter pudding. The pudding can be stored in the fridge for 2-3 days. For best results heat until piping hot before eating.

Cocktails

By Thom Lawson

Mealworm margarita

The mealworms in this recipe replace the cumin I would usually use to make the salt for the rim of my margaritas. This circle of salt is instrumental in making the sweet and sour flavours of the cocktail pop.

For the margarita (makes 1)
- 4 tsp lime juice, plus a lime wedge for coating the glass
- 35ml/1¼fl oz tequila
- 1 tbsp triple sec
- a splash of sugar syrup (see page 172)

For the salt
- mealworms (see recipe)
- salt (see recipe)

01 First, make the salt. Using a spice grinder or mortar and pestle, grind the mealworms down then add the salt, and continue to grind until it is a powder. The ratio should be 3 parts buffalo worms to 1 part salt. Spread the buffalo worm salt out on a plate.
02 Rub the outside of your glass with the lime wedge. This makes the salt stick. Then, tap the rim in the salt until there is a good coating on the outside of the glass.
03 Shake the margarita ingredients over crushed ice in a cocktail shaker.

Serve in the salt-rimmed glass on the rocks or straight up.

The margarita is a classic for a reason and is great served as intended, but there are many little things you can do to tweak it and make it your own. Try a couple of these to get you started.

- Add 2 drops of Tabasco sauce.
- Add 2 teaspoons maraschino liqueur.
- Replace the sugar and triple sec with elderflower liqueur or cordial.
- Shake your ingredients with 2 kaffir lime leaves.

Buffalo worm bloody Mary

Bloody Marys are one of my favourite cocktails to make as they can host all manner of ingredients while retaining their unique flavour. This is an adaptation of my own recipe with the addition of buffalo worms – bloody Marys should be earthy and complex, so the worms are a perfect addition.

For the bloody Mary mix (makes 10)

- 30g/1oz buffalo worms
- 500ml/17fl oz/2 cups tomato juice
- ½ tbsp Dijon mustard
- ½ tbsp English mustard
- 1½ tbsp horseradish
- ¼ bottle Tabasco hot sauce
- 5 tbsp freshly squeezed lemon juice
- ½ bunch of coriander (cilantro) including stems
- salt and freshly ground black pepper, to taste

For the bloody Mary (makes 1)

- 35ml/1¼fl oz vodka
- 50ml/1¾fl oz/scant ¼ cup bloody Mary mix
- about 150ml/5fl oz/⅔ cup tomato juice
- celery sticks
- 1 slice of lemon

01 To make the bloody Mary mix, place all the ingredients in a food processor or blender and blitz together.

02 To make the drink, combine the vodka, bloody Mary mix and tomato juice in a mixing glass and stir well.

Pour over ice and garnish with celery sticks and a slice of lemon.

Cricket flour sours

Sours can be made in many different ways, with many different spirits and all sorts of additions. They are a delicate balance of body, sweetness and sourness. This one uses whisky and cricket flour – the flour adds an interesting texture and nutty depth of flavour.

Serves 2

- 4 tsp sugar syrup (see recipe)
- 35–50ml/1–1¾fl oz whisky
- 1 tsp cricket flour (see page 24)
- 25ml/1fl oz lemon juice
- 1 egg white
- ice cubes
- twist of lemon

01 First, make the sugar syrup. Bring equal quantities of sugar and water to the boil in a heavy-based pan until the sugar has dissolved, then take off the heat and allow to cool.

02 Combine all the ingredients in a cocktail shaker and shake, without ice at this stage – this is known as a dry shake, and it helps the lemon and egg proteins add body to the drink.

03 Open the shaker, add ice cubes, close and shake again.

Strain over ice and garnish with a twist of lemon.

Cricket flour and condensed milk boozy coffee

Chicory has been added to coffee across Europe and the USA for years, originally as a bulking agent when coffee supplies were scarce during the world wars. Nowadays, it's used to give coffee a chocolatey edge and is particularly popular in Italy and New Orleans. This recipe attempts to reproduce the flavour, only using insects. The nuttiness of the cricket flour paired with the sweetness of the condensed milk makes this boozy coffee an excellent digestif.

Serves 2

- 150ml/5fl oz/²/₃ cup condensed milk
- 20g/¾oz/scant ¼ cup cricket flour (see page 24)
- 50ml/1¾fl oz/scant ¼ cup whisky
- 200ml/7fl oz/scant 1 cup filter coffee

01 Heat the condensed milk slowly in a pan, then add the cricket flour and stir in until mixed in.

02 Heat your cups with some boiling water and discard the water, then pour in the whisky and coffee.

Serve the coffee hot with the hot cricket flour and condensed milk mixture on the side. Add to the coffee, stir through and enjoy.

Menu plans

Afternoon tea

Insects and afternoon tea may seem a particularly unusual pairing, but The Ritz is missing a trick. A scone slathered in sweet banana and grasshopper jam and plenty of clotted cream could be your new favourite indulgence. This menu plan gives you a chance to make insect flours and experiment with using them in baking.

- Mum's fat-free mealworm malt loaf *(see page 138)*
- Cricket flour scones with fresh fruit and clotted cream *(see page 140)*
- Sweet banana and grasshopper jam *(see page 161)*
- Cricket flour and condensed milk boozy coffee *(see page 175)*

Alfresco dining

Insects are a great ingredient when making snacks, as well as dips and marinades, meaning they're essential when you're planning an alfresco menu. Start off with a twist on classic nibbles and dips before spicing up your staple of chicken wings and burgers. Melt-in-the-mouth ant-topped caramelised bananas are a delicious finish.

- Mealworm flour tortilla chips with salsa *(see page 49)*
- Spiced grasshopper, butter bean and lime hummus *(see page 120)*
- Mealworm piri-piri whole chicken *(see page 88)*
- Buffalo worm beef burgers with tomato and lime chutney *(see page 108)*
- Grilled bananas with ants, sesame, tamarind and palm sugar caramel *(see page 143)*

A taste of the East

Entomophagy is popular in Thailand, so it's only natural that a lot of our recipes feature the flavours of the East. Turn the below menu into a themed dinner for friends as a way of introducing them to insect ingredients. Or try the recipes for buffalo worm green and red curry pastes (pages 126 and 129), or the mealworm satay sauce on page 132, to create your own dishes.

- Insect chilli salts with sour fruits *(see page 62)*
- Grasshopper, prawn and ginger spring rolls *(see page 82)*
- Curried beer tempura grasshoppers *(see page 73)*
- Creamy mealworm and coconut noodles *(see page 95)*
- Insect chimp stick *(see page 155)*

Sunday brunch

This menu is perfect for a lazy Sunday morning and a big appetite. These recipes are also jam-packed with protein (thanks to our many-legged friends), which is known to work wonders for a hangover or simply give you a boost at the start of the day. Wake yourself up with a stiff bloody Mary and get cooking!

- Buffalo worm bloody Mary *(see page 170)*
- Grasshopper and maltose porridge *(see page 52)*
- Josh's scrambled eggs, mullet roe and ants *(see page 80)*
- Double cheese mealworm rarebit with soft-boiled duck egg *(see page 64)*

Farming and sourcing

With the rise of entomophagy has come the emergence of farms dedicated to rearing the mini-livestock. Grub supports The Border Consortium in Thailand, an organisation providing Burmese refugees with food, shelter and a source of income, of which one is a cricket-rearing project. Crickets provide the impoverished families in these camps with a tasty and nutritious ingredient as well as the opportunity to sell the surplus at market. A win-win solution.

Far left: A cricket farm in Thanon Nang Klarn village in Nakhon Ratchasima province, Thailand. It's one of many family businesses in this village where farmers rear crickets in their backyards to meet local demand. Left: Plates of fried insects, including crickets and grasshoppers, for sale at a local market in Vientiane, Laos

Rearing insects has taken off in the West, too. It makes sense: as the price of feed for traditional livestock increases, insects provide an alternative and sustainable source of income for farmers (more about that on page 14). In the US, more than 100 tonnes of insects are farmed each year, although producers are struggling to satisfy increasing demand.

Cricket farming is still in its infancy and the companies turning it into a business are often learning on the job. Having opened the first dedicated cricket farm in the UK, Grub has first-hand experience of this. But it's encouraging to see that farming techniques are constantly improving as the demand grows. Next Millennium Farms in Canada is one enterprise dedicated to the cause. In the UK, Grub works with Entovista to rear crickets and make ready-to-use cricket flour. Together with an experienced and passionate entomologist we've built a bespoke facility to rear a happy and healthy orchestra of crickets. As much as possible, we've tried to replicate their natural environment, although we've added our own little touches too – for example, crickets love roosting in the nooks and crannies of upturned egg cartons, so we have plenty of these. Our crickets are reared specifically for human consumption and are fed a combination of high quality grains, carrots and potatoes. And they're kept in a very clean environment, under highly controlled environmental conditions to make sure the very best and most nutritious crickets are farmed. You should hear the noise they make, it's incredible – just like being on a tropical holiday (but in Cumbria)!

Our farmed crickets (along with the other insects used in our recipes) can be purchased through our website at **www.eatgrub.co.uk** and we are able to ship worldwide. There is also a growing number of online stores that stock ready-to-eat insects, though they vary wildly in quality and we recommend using a trusted, ethical supplier.

Index

Index

Index

Acknowledgements

We would like to say a huge thank you to all our friends and families for supporting us in our Grub venture, even those who thought we were a little crazy when we said we wanted to start our own edible insect company!

Thanks to Jay Radia for helping us with initial funding for Grub, and a special mention to Helen Radia and Karen and Roy Whippey for their unconditional love. Thanks also to Sinead Groves and Max Hargreaves for allowing Seb to constantly cover the kitchen walls, ceilings and floors with bugs until the early hours of the morning (all in the name of culinary experimentation).

Thanks to Seb's mum Vicky Fossaluzza for her unwavering support, both in attending all of our pop-ups and never being afraid to lend a hand (and her kitchen!), as well as Craig Broadhurst for his help over the years.

Thanks to chef Andy Oliver for bringing Seb and Grub together, and Anita Potter for helping out when shit was hitting the fan and for being the 'boss'!

Thanks to Poonum Chauhan for designing our brand and Chloe Marshall for her copy writing for Grub.

We would also like to thank everyone that has worked so hard to make the Eat Grub cookbook a reality.

Thanks to Zena Alkayat for believing in Grub and for her singleminded passion for creating an awesome insect-inspired cookbook!

Thanks to Glenn Howard for the book design, Mowie Kay for photography, Olivia Bennett for prop styling, Hat Margolies from Lucid for helping bring the team together, Kathy Steer for recipe editing and Euan Ferguson for proof reading.

A huge thanks to Thom Lawson who came up with the amazing insect-packed cocktail recipes. And to Howard Bell, Entovista Research Director, for input into the farming section.

Thanks also to Dr George McGavin for the mealworm loaf recipe and Josh Pollen of Blanch & Shock for the scrambled egg and ant recipe. And a final thanks to Carl-Daniel Smith at Forager Ltd for sourcing those delicious ants.